The 901 BEST JOKES There Ever Was

(Plus Quite A Few Second Best)

The 901 BEST JOKES There Ever Was

(Plus Quite a Few Second Best)

Written, Edited, Compiled, and Stolen
by

J. R. Miller

Rutledge Hill Press®
Nashville, Tennessee
A Thomas Nelson Company

Published by Rutledge Hill Press, a Thomas Nelson Company, P.O. Box 141000, Nashville, Tennessee 37214.

Typography by Compass Communications, Inc., Nashville, Tennessee
Design by Harriette Bateman

Library of Congress Cataloging-in-Publication Data

Miller, J. R., 1938–
    The 901 best jokes there ever was (plus quite a few second best) / written, edited, compiled, and stolen by J. R. Miller.
      p. cm.
    ISBN 1-55853-122-X
    I. Title. II. Title: Nine hundred one best jokes there ever was.
III. Title: Nine hundred and one best jokes there ever was.
PN6162.M49 1991
818'.5402—dc20   91-24866
                                                              CIP

Printed in the United States of America
14 15 16 PHX 05 04 03 02

To Nita, Moonie, and Bob

Introduction

After years of writing comedy material for television shows, stand-up comics, magazines, etc., I naturally built an impressive file of funny jokes and ideas as reference material. One of the results of this ongoing search for ideas in every nook and cranny available—including every joke book I could get my hands on—was to develop a clear notion of what was required to write the world's best joke book.

So I did.

Whether you're reading this material for nothing more than entertainment or using it as research to punch up your own "act," you're going to love this book.

I've cut to the chase with this stuff. Each bit has been carefully edited for comic value, then checked for brevity. You will find no chickens crossing any roads in this book, only very few—funny—talking animals, and a minimum of cutesy kids' stuff. There are no limericks and only a handful of puns.

The jokes here are organized in alphabetical order, but be advised that doesn't mean much if you are looking for material concerning a particular subject. If you have reason to need a joke about a specific topic, don't limit your search to only that subject. Jokes can almost always be edited and re-written to address entirely different themes. Check the index for related topics.

How to "Spin" a Joke

When I re-work a joke to address a different subject, I call it "spinning" the joke. A recent such "spin" I did can be used as a good illustration of how to re-write an old premise into a new joke.

My friend, country comedian Phil Campbell, is the son of the late "Hee-Haw" star, Archie Campbell, and I wanted to build something for Phil that insiders could spot as an acknowledgment of his father's influence.

I first met Phil while I was writing the sitcom "I-40 Paradise" for Elmer Alley at the Nashville Network and Cinetel Productions in Knoxville. Phil became a regular cast member of "I-40 Paradise," then of "Hee-Haw" in 1990. For Phil, I "spun" a classic sketch that Archie had originally built to go somewhat like this. . . .

Archie: "Roy, did you hear about Freddy Wilson deciding to be a crop duster airplane pilot?"

Roy: "No, I didn't, Archie. That's good."

Archie: "No, that's bad. He was learning to fly when his airplane caught fire and he had to jump."

Roy: "Whoa! That's bad!"

Archie: "No, that's good. He was wearing a parachute."

Roy: "Oh, that's good."

Archie: "No, that's bad. The parachute didn't open."

Roy: "Oh! That is definitely bad!"

Archie: "No, that was good. He just happened to jump out right over a farmer's big ol' soft haystack."

Roy: "Oh! That's good!"

Archie: "No, that was bad. As he was falling, he spotted a pitchfork in the middle of the haystack."

Roy: "Oh-oh! That's bad!!"

Archie: "No, that was good. As it turned out, he missed the pitchfork."

Roy: "Now, Archie, I know that's good!"

Archie: "No, Roy, that wasn't good, either. He missed the haystack."

* * *

For Phil, I "spun" this wonderful "That's-Good-No-That's-Bad" classic into a fellow trying to get to his hotel from the airport in a broken taxi:

Irlene: "Phil, I heard you flew to California on vacation. I'll bet that was great!"

Phil: "No, Irlene, that was bad. When I got there, I missed the bus from the airport to my hotel."

Irlene: "Oh, that's bad."

Phil: "No, that wasn't too bad. I finally got a taxi, and the driver was real friendly."

Irlene: "That's good."

Phil: "No, that was bad. The transmission in the taxi broke before we even got away from the airport."

Irlene: "Oh, that's bad!"

Phil: "No, that was good. Turned out, reverse gear still worked, so we weren't altogether stranded."

Irlene: "Oh, that's good!"

Phil: "No, that was bad. The driver decided to drive me all the way to my hotel, backwards."

Irlene: "Whoa! That's bad!"

Phil: "No, that was good."

Irlene: "It was?"

Phil: "Yep. When we finally did get to the hotel, the driver owed me six dollars and forty cents."

This easy adaptability of most jokes is generally good, but it can make sorting them into categories—alphabetical or otherwise—a real pain in the butt. Look at this joke:

"Could you spare five dollars to help bury a rap musician?"
"Here's ten . . . bury two of 'em."

That's a joke about rap musicians, of course, but it's also a joke about borrowing money, loaning money, funerals, and, perhaps most of all, prejudice.

Notice that the rap musician could just as easily be a member of any group at which the joke-teller wants to poke fun.

The dead fellow may as well have been a tax collector, a politician, a TV game show host, Jew, Irishman, etc . . . even a mother-in-law.

"Could you spare five dollars to help me pay for my mother-in-law's funeral?"

"Here's a ten-dollar bill. Bury mine while you're at it."

Same basic joke, different "spin." Check this joke:

A fellow noticed that his next door neighbor, an attorney, rode a bicycle to the commuter station every morning while the lawyer's wife ran along behind, panting, sweating, struggling to keep up.

Finally, the fellow asked the lawyer, "Tell me . . . how come you get to ride that bicycle every morning, but your wife has to run along behind?"

"Simple," the lawyer shrugged. "She doesn't have a bicycle."

As with the joke about the rap musician, it's obvious that the lawyer in this joke could be someone from any profession, race, or religious group.

But you could go further. The bicycle could be a farm tractor, for example, with which a farmer could be plowing while his wife plows another part of the field with a mule . . . "because she ain't got a tractor."

I've changed countless numbers of jokes in just such a way to make them "fit" whatever I was writing at the time. Dirty jokes have become jokes about kissing, racist jokes have become jokes about politicians, etc.

I've already "spun" and used that last joke as a moonshiner hauling jugs of whiskey in a wheelbarrow. His wife, of course, had to struggle along behind with an equal number of jugs on her back . . . "because she ain't got a wheelbarrow."

So alphabetizing jokes into particular categories can be a lesson in futility. Nevertheless, it does furnish a starting point from which to begin searching for just the right joke.

Be Sure the "Thump" Is at the End

If you enjoy telling jokes, or if you're using this book as reference material to punch up your writing or a speech you're scheduled to make, you should be conscious of the most widespread mistake made when telling a joke.

In every joke there's a punch line at the end, of course; but within that punch line there is almost always a particular key word or phrase that should come at the very end of the punch line itself. This word or phrase carries the revelatory surprise—the "thump" of realization—that comprises the very heart of the joke.

Be sure this "thump" word or phrase is at the very end. The most common way to ruin a joke is to add words after that "thump." That moonshiner joke above, for example, wouldn't be as strong if the moonshiner's wife had to carry those jugs on her back ". . . because I got a wheelbarrow and she don't have one." All those extra words serve to soften the surprise of the "thump" and weaken the joke. The soul of a good joke contains the element of surprise, of sudden revelation, and the degree of care with which you deliver that revelation can determine the success of the joke.

—J. R. Miller

The
901
BEST
JOKES
There
Ever
Was

(Plus Quite A Few Second Best)

Adam & Eve

He: Why do you insist that Adam and Eve had to be from West
Virginia?
She: Simple. They had no house, no car, no job, but they still
thought they were living in Paradise.

★ ★ ★

Sunday School Teacher: Miss Johnson, could you tell the rest
of our Sunday school class the name of the very first man?
Miss Johnson: Yes, I could, but I promised I wouldn't.

Advertising

"My daughter's new boyfriend is in subliminal advertising."
"Have you met him yet?"
"Yes, but only for a split second."

Age

"Do you mean to tell me your whole family was shocked and
surprised when your ninety-five-year-old uncle died?"
"That's right."
"But, if he was ninety-five-years-old, why was everybody
surprised?"
"Because his parachute didn't open."

★ ★ ★

"Grandpa, don't you hope doctors will find a way to let us get younger?"
"At my age, I just hope they can let us get older."

★ ★ ★

At her age, a see-through nightgown won't help.
None of her boyfriends can see through it.

★ ★ ★

When we first met, she and I were the same age.

★ ★ ★

Research shows, the best way to live longer is to stop doing everything that makes you want to.

★ ★ ★

Nurse to Patient: How old are you, Mrs. Smith?
Patient: None of your business.
Nurse: But the doctor must know your age for his records.
Patient: Well, first, multiply twenty by two, then add ten. Got that?
Nurse: Yes. Fifty.
Patient: All right, now subtract fifty, and tell me, what do you get?
Nurse: Zero.
Patient: Right. And that's exactly the chance of me telling you my age.

★ ★ ★

The news reporter asked the one hundred-five-year-old man's advice on how to live to such a ripe old age.
The old man answered, "Nothin' to it. Just drink at least one shot of whiskey every day."
"But lots of people drink whiskey every day," the reporter said, "and yet they die long before they reach old age. How do you explain that?"

"Simple," the old man shrugged, "they don't keep doing it long enough."

★ ★ ★

Teacher to Third Grade Student: Jimmy, if both of your parents were born in 1965, how old would they say they are now?
Jimmy: That depends.
Teacher: It does? Depends on what?
Jimmy: On if you ask my father or my mother.

★ ★ ★

The difference between an old bull and a young bull is that a young bull will spot a bunch of cows at the other end of a pasture and run right down and bother a couple of them. An old bull will walk down and bother them all.

★ ★ ★

You know you're old if you can remember when bacon, eggs, and sunshine were good for you.

★ ★ ★

"Have you lived around here all your life?"
"Not yet."

★ ★ ★

"Tell me, how did you end up here?"
"Oh, I haven't ended up yet."

★ ★ ★

"She claims her thirty-ninth birthday isn't far off!"
"Well, it isn't; it was only five or six years ago."

★ ★ ★

Airlines

First Young Woman: I'm going to be an airline flight attendant because it's a wonderful way to meet lots of men.
Second Young Woman: Oh, there are plenty of other jobs where you could meet men.
First Young Woman: Maybe so, but they wouldn't be strapped in their seats.

★ ★ ★

Passenger to Airline Ticket Agent: I want my brown suitcase sent to Los Angeles, my green suitcase sent to Kansas City, and my tan suitcase sent to New Orleans.
Ticket Agent: I'm sorry, sir; this flight is to Nashville. We can't do that.
Passenger: Why not? You did it last time.

★ ★ ★

Pilot to Flight Attendant: Bring me some cotton balls for my ears.
Flight Attendant: Does the roar of the engines hurt your ears?
Pilot: No, but all the screaming will when I announce we've lost our landing gear.

★ ★ ★

She: Isn't that the airline with the poor safety record?
He: I'll say! Last week, two of their flight simulators collided.

★ ★ ★

Passenger: Stewardess, why are we flying so low?
Flight Attendant: Nothing to worry about, sir. The radar's broken, and the captain's following the highway signs.

★ ★ ★

The flight attendant announced to the passengers that the four-engined aircraft had lost an engine, but she quickly assured them the plane could easily fly with three engines.

"The only thing is," she said, "we'll be about an hour late arriving."

A few minutes later, she announced that they had lost a second engine, but she assured everyone that the aircraft could fly with only two engines.

"But," she said, "our arrival will be delayed about two and a half hours."

Later, she had to announce that they were losing a third engine. Again, she assured everyone that there was no reason to worry. The aircraft could fly with only one engine.

"But we won't arrive now," she said, "until five hours later than scheduled."

"Nuts!" a passenger said. "With my luck, we'll lose that last engine and be stuck up here all night."

★ ★ ★

Flight Attendant to Passengers: Attention, please! The pilot has asked me to announce that he has good news and bad news.

Anxious Passenger: What's the bad news?

Flight Attendant: The bad news is, we're lost.

Passenger: Lost?! Then what in the world can be the good news?!

Flight Attendant: The good news is, we're way ahead of schedule.

★ ★ ★

Angry Passenger to Luggage Claims Clerk: If this airline can fly three thousand miles from New York City and find Los Angeles in the dark, why can't they find my luggage?

★ ★ ★

Passenger: Stewardess, how often does this airline fly to Nashville?

Flight Attendant: Oh, about every third try.

★ ★ ★

Flight Attendant to Passengers: I'm happy to announce that all passengers can pick up their bags as usual. The strike by the baggage handlers has been postponed. . . . They lost their picket signs.

★ ★ ★

The passengers were exiting the plane after landing, and one smiling, satisfied passenger paused to congratulate the flight attendant.

"Stewardess," he said happily, "I want to compliment you and the crew and especially the captain for getting here right on time. It's not often that an airline gets to where it's going exactly when they claim it will. I'm going to call your home office and let them know how pleased I am."

"Why, thank you, sir," the flight attendant answered, "but I think you should know—this is yesterday's flight."

★ ★ ★

Passenger: Stewardess, what time does this plane get to Atlanta?

Flight Attendant: I'm not sure; we've never made it before.

★ ★ ★

"Those big airplanes seem to crash a lot."

"No, they don't. They almost never crash more than once."

Animals

"I want you to come out to my place and ride my new horse."

"But I've never ridden a horse."

"Then you'll be starting even. This horse has never been ridden."

★ ★ ★

"I heard that your pet skunk doesn't know how to swim."

"That's true. He jumped in the creek and stank to the bottom."

★ ★ ★

"My neighbor's mad because my dog knows how to fetch the evening paper."

"Why would that make your neighbor angry?"

"I don't subscribe to the paper."

★ ★ ★

"Is it true that you play checkers every week with your neighbor's dog?"

"Yep."

"Wow! That must be a very smart dog!"

"Naw. I beat him three out of four."

★ ★ ★

A fellow took his talking dog to a show business talent agent, and the dog told six or eight familiar old jokes, including a couple with French and English accents.

"What do you think?" the dog s owner asked the agent. "We're gonna make a fortune, right?"

"Well," the agent replied, "his delivery's all right, but his material's weak."

★ ★ ★

"What was that terrible animal howling all night? I couldn't sleep a wink."

"That was a timber wolf."

"Impossible. There aren't any timber wolves around here."

"I know. That's exactly what he keeps howling about."

★ ★ ★

"This morning, when I went for the mail, I found a turtle in the middle of the road."

"I wonder what it was doing there?"

"Oh, about one-fourth mile per hour."

* * *

"My billy goat ate my videotape of *Gone With the Wind*."
"Did he get sick?"
"No, but he didn't like it as well as the book."

* * *

The salesman came through the gate toward the old man sitting on the porch when a large dog came growling and snarling from under the house.

"Hey, Old Timer," the salesman said, stopping in his tracks. "Is that dog safe?"

"Well," replied the old man, "I'd say he's a danged sight safer than you are."

* * *

"Is it true that you entered an eleven-year-old horse in the Kentucky Derby?"

"Yep."

"But why in the world would anyone enter an eleven-year-old horse in the Kentucky Derby?"

"Well, for the first ten years, we couldn't catch him."

* * *

Upon entering the little country grocery store, the stranger noticed a sign saying, *Danger! Beware of Dog!* posted on the door glass.

Inside, he noticed a harmless old hound dog asleep on the floor near the cash register. He asked the store's owner, "Is that the dog folks are supposed to beware of?"

"Yep," the proprietor answered. "That's him."

The stranger couldn't help being amused. "That certainly doesn't look like a dangerous dog to me," he chuckled. "Why in the world did you decide to post that sign?"

"Because," the owner replied, "before I posted that sign, people kept tripping over him."

* * *

"Can you tell me one of the most popular uses for cow-hide?"

"Sure; it holds cows together."

★ ★ ★

"Is it true that a charging bull won't hurt you if you carry a piece of fruit?"

"That depends on how fast you carry it."

★ ★ ★

Where do baby storks come from?

Antiques

Young Boy to Mother: Y'know that antique vase you said has been handed down in our family from one generation to the next, generation after generation?

Mother: Yes?

Boy: Well, my generation dropped it.

Aquariums

To describe an aquarium, it's best not to be a fish.

Armed Forces

"You say the war ruined your life?"

"That's right. It sure did."

"But you were never in the armed forces."

"No, but my wife's first husband was killed in action."

★ ★ ★

Wife to Husband: Did you see those soldiers looking at that beautiful young girl that just walked past?
Husband: What soldiers?

★ ★ ★

Lieutenant to Private: Hey, soldier, why are you carrying only one bucket while everyone else is carrying two buckets?
Private: Sir, I guess those other guys are too lazy to make two trips.

★ ★ ★

"When you were in the army, did they give you a commission?"
"Naw. . . . just a straight salary like everybody else."

★ ★ ★

"When my brother joined the army, we knew the war would be over in no time at all."
"Why's that?"
"Because my brother hasn't held a job more than two weeks in his whole life."

★ ★ ★

"Nobody'd want my wife in the armed forces."
"Why not?"
"Because everytime somebody yelled 'Charge!' she'd run for the mall."

★ ★ ★

The sergeant came into the barracks to rouse the new recruits from their sleep.
"Awright!" he bawled, "Up and at 'em! It's four-thirty!"
"If it's four-thirty, sergeant," a recruit answered sleepily, "you'd better get to bed. We got a busy day tomorrow."

★ ★ ★

"When you were in the navy, did they decorate you?"
"No, but they kept me cleaned up pretty good."

Astrology

First Young Woman: Is it true you broke up with that good-looking new boyfriend of yours?
Second Young Woman: Yes. We're just not at all compatible. I'm a Libra, and he's a Tightwad.

★ ★ ★

★ Astrology for Today ★

Aquarius (*January 20–February 18*)
You are inventive and imaginative, which explains your habitual lying. Because Aquarians have no sex appeal whatsoever, they are fortunate to have no sexual drive. Of course, everyone regards you as being dense, but you never notice. Your idea of fine food usually involves some form of hot dogs. Inherent dishonesty may cause problems in P.M.

Pisces (*February 19–March 20*)
Your idea that you are attractive to the opposite sex is rooted in your vivid imagination. The rest of us laugh a lot about that. Research shows there are twice as many Piscean jokes as Polish jokes, but you, of course, are not aware of that. Hair in nose presents social handicap in P.M. Good day to practice alphabet.

Aries (*March 21–April 19*)
You are loyal, hard working, and trustworthy, which helps explain why you are a minimum wage flunky. You have no special skills not involving a broom. Most likely, you drive a used Camaro with empty Burger King sacks under the front seats. Avoid wearing swimsuit until very late P.M.

Taurus (*April 20–May 20*)
You are persistent and determined when striving for a goal, but have no clue how to achieve it. All your friends pretend not to notice your lack of intelligence—at least to your face. Research shows that if Taureans were not counted in student tests, grade point averages in this country would rise 4.5 percent. A.M. good time to quit school.

Gemini (*May 21–June 20*)

You are extraordinarily intelligent and articulate, and those around you appreciate intelligence in someone so ugly. Geminis are known to become more repulsive as they grow older; future looks bleak. You are known among co-workers as "Horse Face." P.M. best time for plastic surgery; A.M. good time to buy breath mints wholesale.

Cancer (*June 21–July 22*)

You are conservative and against taking risks. This makes you the dullest person in your circle of friends (if you have any friends), especially considering your utter lack of ambition and/or imagination. There has never been a Cancer who has amounted to anything. Ignore your fantasy of meeting Pat Sajak in person, since he wouldn't like you either. P.M. don't miss Tournament of Champions on "Family Feud."

Leo (*July 23–August 22*)

You are compassionate, understanding, and sympathetic; that's why you are known among friends as a sucker. Your parents secretly gave your brothers and sisters hundreds of toys, and while you slept the rest of the family ate meat. You wore hand-me-downs even though you were the oldest child. Tomorrow P.M. check career opportunities at McDonald's.

Virgo (*August 23–September 22*)

Virgos are clever and able to achieve notoriety; that's why your friends regard you as a self-centered boor. You most likely have never watched a PBS program, but if you did, you didn't understand it. If you were at all likeable, friends would pity you; as it is, no one ever thinks about you. No Virgo has ever been elected to public office. A.M. best time for sulking.

Libra (*September 23–October 22*)

You are shrewd in business matters and can usually get your way with others. That's why everyone despises you. Closest friends enjoy having parties that are kept secret from you. Co-workers often mimic your poor posture. Even Dale Carnegie wouldn't like you. P.M. good time to commit fraud you've been considering.

Scorpio (*October 23–November 21*)

You are optimistic, enthusiastic, and ambitious. Too bad you have no talent. Most Scorpios end up in prison or on welfare, and it has been documented that all Scorpios have husbands or wives who cheat. There has never been a Scorpio with a successful marriage, and all Scorpios have less-than-average children. P.M. best time to spy on spouse.

Sagittarius (*November 22–December 21*)
You are artistic and imaginative, but that stems from your warped view of reality. Very few people admit to being a Sagittarian, but the rest of us know who you are because all Sagittarians are left-handed. If you are not left-handed, your mother has lied to you about your birthdate as part of a cover-up. A.M. good time to search for real father.

Capricorn (*December 22–January 19*)
Capricorns can often be trained to be fairly good bus drivers and reasonably successful shoe sales clerks, but they cannot be taught to succeed at personal relationships. You probably have no social plans for the weekend anyway, but if so, they will result in disaster. It is unfortunate that Capricorns have no sex appeal to go along with their inordinately powerful sex drive. P.M. good time to rent videos.

Athletes

"I hear your cousin used to be a good athlete."
"He sure was. When he was a kid, he could climb two trees at once."

★ ★ ★

"My cousin runs five miles a day, doesn't eat sweets, red meat or dairy products, sleeps at least eight hours a night, doesn't drink or smoke, never drinks coffee or soda pop, and never goes out in direct sunlight."
"Someday he's going to feel like a fool."
"A fool?"
"That's right. How's he going to explain lying in bed, dying of nothing?"

Auctions

First Farmer: I gotta go; I'm taking my wife and her mother to the hog auction.
Second Farmer: How much do you think they'll bring?

Automobiles

One good thing about having so many cars—there's been a lot less horse stealing.

★ ★ ★

Texan: Back in Texas, I can get in my car and drive all morning before I come to the end of my property.
Redneck: I know how you feel. I got a car just like that.

★ ★ ★

"I understand that car of yours is the oldest car in the county."
"I guess it is . . . the last time I bought plates for it, they gave me uppers and lowers."

★ ★ ★

"Yesterday, I got a real nice used car for my wife."
"I know your wife. It sounds like you got a good deal."

★ ★ ★

"I want my money back on the car you sold me."
"How come?"
"Everything on that car makes noise except the horn."

★ ★ ★

Angry Car Buyer: I want my money back! You said that car you sold me was just like new!
Car Seller: It had to be. I only drove it when I could get it started.

★ ★ ★

"That used car battery you sold me for five dollars didn't even last two months."
"Well, the five dollars didn't even last two days."

★ ★ ★

Angry Car Buyer: When you sold me that car, you said it was a one-owner.
Car Dealer: That's right. You didn't ask if it was a taxi company.

★ ★ ★

"Of all the stupid things you've ever done, locking the cat in the trunk of the car has to be the dumbest!"
"Oh, yeah? Wait'll you ask about your car keys."

Auto Racing

"Is it true your cousin lost his job as a race car driver because he was stupid?"
"Yep. He kept pulling into the pits to ask directions."

Banks

"I hear the First National Bank is looking for a new teller."
"I thought they just hired a new teller last week."
"Right. That's the one they're looking for."

★ ★ ★

"I went to the bank at two o'clock this afternoon, but they were closed."
"So?"
"So, there's a sign on the door that says, '9 to 5'."
"That's not their business hours. That's the odds on whether they'll be open tomorrow."

Bars/Bartenders

A pink squirrel hopped onto a barstool and squeaked out in a clear voice, "Bartender! Service here!"

The bartender was astounded. "Hey!" the bartender said, "Do you know there's a drink named after you?"

"What?" the pink squirrel replied, "There's a drink named Fred?"

★ ★ ★

"Bartender, was I in this bar last night, and did I spend twenty dollars?"

"Yeah."

"That's a relief! I was afraid I'd lost it."

—W. C. Fields

★ ★ ★

The drunk entered the bar, seated himself on a barstool, and called to the bartender: "Give me a drink, barkeep! Give everybody in the place a drink, and give yourself a drink, too!"

After everyone—including the bartender—had downed their drinks, the drunk again ordered for everyone: "Bartender! Give me another drink. Give everyone in the place another drink, and give yourself another drink!"

"Wait a minute," said the bartender. "I think you'd better pay for that first round of drinks before you buy another."

"Oh," said the drunk, "I don't have any money."

Not surprisingly, the barkeep got mad. He grabbed the drunk, dragged him out the back door into the alley, and beat him up.

Ten minutes later, the drunk re-entered through the front door, re-seated himself, and said to the bartender, "Bartender, give me a drink, and give everyone in the place a drink."

"Humph!" answered the bartender sarcastically. "What about me? Don't I get one, too?"

"Noooo," said the drunk. "You get mean when you drink."

★ ★ ★

"There are almost a hundred bars in this town, and I've never set foot in one of them."
"Which one is that?"

Baseball

Baseball: Twelve minutes of excitement crammed into two-and-a-half hours.

★ ★ ★

Restaurant Hostess to Restaurant Manager: There's a base-ball umpire on the telephone. He wants to make dinner reservations for himself and two friends.
Restaurant Manager: Hang up. It's a crank call. There's no such thing as a baseball umpire with two friends.

★ ★ ★

"What do Michael Jackson and the Atlanta Braves have in common?"
"They both wear a glove on one hand for no apparent reason."

Batteries

I bought some batteries, but they weren't included. I tried to return them and get my money back, but I didn't have them because they weren't included in the first place. I had to buy them all over again.

Beauticians/Beauty Shops

Beautician to Customer: How'd you like the beautician who filled in while I was on vacation?
Customer: Well, she was a gossip, she made my face look blotchy, and she nearly ruined my hair. It was like you never left.

★ ★ ★

Woman to Beautician: When you're finished with me, will my husband think I'm beautiful?
Beautician: Maybe. Does he still drink a lot?

Beauty Contests

They had a beauty contest in my old neighborhood, and nobody won.

★ ★ ★

She entered the Miss America Contest, and they tried to have her deported.

★ ★ ★

"My sister's going to enter the Miss Professional Golfing Association Beauty Contest."
"What's her handicap?"

Bigamy

"My wife's uncle was nearly executed for bigamy."
"Are you crazy? We don't execute people for bigamy."
"We don't—but tell that to his two wives."

★ ★ ★

"A man with two wives is called a bigamist, but what do you call a man with more than two wives?"
"A pigamist."

★ ★ ★

"When a man has more than one wife, they call it 'bigamy'. What do they call it if a woman has more than one husband?"
"Insanity."

★ ★ ★

The worst thing about bigamy is, you get two mothers-in-law.

Birds

"I want my money back on that canary you sold me!"
"Why? What's the trouble?"
"That bird's only got one leg."
"I know that."
"If you know that, gimme back my money!"
"Listen, you told me you wanted a bird that was a good singer, and that's the best singer I got. If you wanted a dancer, you should've said so!"

—Flip Wilson

★ ★ ★

"Hey, look at dem poity boids!"
"Those aren't 'boids'; those are 'birds'."
"Is dat right? Gee, dey sure look like boids."

★ ★ ★

Two vultures had been sitting atop a high cliff for hours, scanning the earth below in vain for carrion.
Finally, one turned to the other in exasperation and said, "Patience, my fanny. I'm gonna kill something."

★ ★ ★

While vacationing in the wilds of Arizona, a fellow met a hermit who had taught a chicken to speak English and Spanish. After a lot of haggling, the guy managed to buy the chicken and had it shipped home to his wife.

Days later, when he'd reached a telephone, he called his wife to make sure the chicken had arrived safely.

"Yes, it did," his wife answered. "We had it for supper last night."

"You ate it?!" he screamed. "Listen, that was stupid! That chicken was going to make us rich! That chicken could speak two different languages!"

"If it could speak two different languages," his wife asked, "why didn't it speak up when it saw me with the ax?"

Birthdays

His parents keep reading his birth certificate—looking for loopholes.

★ ★ ★

First Gossip: Say, Martha's wearing a beautiful coat this evening.
Second Gossip: Yes, her husband bought her that coat for her thirty-ninth birthday.
First Gossip: Well, it certainly has held up well.

★ ★ ★

"Are you going to Sally's thirty-ninth birthday party?"
"Sure. I go every year."

Blind Dates

First Young Man: That blind date you fixed me up with must work in a stable.

Second Young Man: What makes you say that?
First Young Man: At dinner, I saw her flick away a fly with her ears.

★ ★ ★

"Where'd you take that blind date I fixed you up with last night?"
"I took her to the football game."
"But that was the coldest night of the year. Did you enjoy yourself?"
"No. The whole time we were there, her tooth chattered."

★ ★ ★

First Young Woman: Did anything exciting happen with your blind date last night?
Second Young Woman: Yeah, his guide dog bit me.

★ ★ ★

First Young Man: You say your blind date last night was pretty ugly, huh?
Second Young Man: Ugly?! At dinner, she had to sneak up on her glass to get a drink.

Books

Fred: I'm turning over a new leaf. I just finished reading a book called *One Hundred And One Easy Ways To Make Money.*
Ed: Sounds good. Then maybe people won't think of you as being so lazy.
Fred: Right. You're looking at a new man. I'm on my way to the top. Say, could you loan me ten dollars?
Ed: What? You just finished a book called *One Hundred And One Easy Ways to Make Money*, and now you want to borrow ten dollars?!
Fred: Yeah. That's one of the easiest ways.

★ ★ ★

If some folks want to read about love and marriage, they have to buy two separate books.

★ ★ ★

Ed: If you were trapped on a deserted island and had only one book to read, what would be the title of that book?
Fred: How To Build A Good Boat.

Boxing/Boxers

A drunk wandered into a neighborhood gym and spotted a boxer shadow-boxing in the center of the boxing ring.

He watched the boxer dancing and punching the air for a while, then called to him, "Hey! You might as well quit fighting, pal. He's gone!"

★ ★ ★

"Why do they call your cousin, the heavyweight boxer, 'Submarine Jones'?"
"Because he's always taking a dive."

★ ★ ★

"I hear your uncle used to be a professional boxer."
"Yep. He went by the name of 'Sweet Chariot Johnson.'"
"That seems like a strange name for a boxer."
"Not really. He was always swinging low."

★ ★ ★

"Your opponent in the upcoming fight is ten years younger than you, eight inches taller than you, and forty pounds heavier than you. What do you consider your biggest advantage?"
"I got him scared."
"Scared?"
"Yeah, he's scared he's gonna kill me."

★ ★ ★

"You won your last fight in only six rounds. Did you think it would be over so fast?"

"It would've been shorter if I hadn't had sweat blurring my vision."

"Your vision?"

"Uh-huh. If I could've seen better, I wouldn't have wasted so many punches on the referee."

★ ★ ★

"You won your last fight in less than five rounds. What do you believe was your biggest advantage?"

"Well, I call it my famous 'Three-Legged' punch."

"Your 'Three-Legged' punch?"

"Yeah. I hit him with my stool."

Builders/Contractors

"Did you know it took almost a hundred years to build just one pyramid?"

"Must be the same contractor that remodeled my bathroom."

★ ★ ★

"I'd like to buy some two-by-fours."

"How long do you want 'em?"

"For a pretty good while. I'm building a garage."

Business

The businessman called his less-than-ambitious son into his office and announced he had decided to make him a full partner in the company.

"Which part of the company would you like to be in charge of, son?" he asked.

"Well," the son answered, "I don't like working in the shipping room, and I don't like being in sales, and I'd rather not be in the bookkeeping department—"

"Listen," the father said, "as a full partner, what would you like the most?"

"Hmmm," the son pondered, "I guess, most of all, I'd like you to buy me out."

★ ★ ★

"Some businessman! He lost everything when he invested in Frederick's of Baghdad."

Cajuns

"What's the difference between cajun food and creole food?"

"Cajun food's been dead longer."

Camping

"I hear you got lost camping and it took your friends two days to find you."

"That's right."

"Don't you know when you get lost in the wilds, you're supposed to fire three shots in the air?"

"I did that. It didn't help."

"Well, if it doesn't help the first time, you're supposed to fire three more shots in the air."

"I did that, too. In fact, I kept firing until I ran out of arrows."

★ ★ ★

First Woman: I understand your husband got upset because you lost the compass while the two of you were camping?

Second Woman: No, he wasn't upset because the compass was lost. He was upset because we were lost.

★ ★ ★

I got my uncle a seven-piece camping outfit for his birthday
. . . a sleeping bag and a six-pack.

Celebrities

"I heard you got into a big argument with a fellow last night
about giving him your autograph."
"Yeah, but he finally took it."

★ ★ ★

"Loan me a quarter; I want to call one of my fans."
"Here's fifty cents. Call both of them."

Chances

How come "slim chance" and "fat chance" mean the same
thing?"

Cheerleaders

First Cheerleader: What took you so long to take that note to
   the football coach?
Second Cheerleader: He was in the locker room with the
   team.
First Cheerleader: Oh, and you had to wait until he came out
   to give it to him?
Second Cheerleader: No, I took it right in.
First Cheerleader: Into the men's locker room?! Don't you
   know better than to go into a men's locker room?!
Second Cheerleader: I do now.

Cities and Towns

Our town is so small . . .

. . . the amusement park's got only one bumper car.

. . . the biggest shopping center is three pickups backed up to the highway.

. . . we've got a four way stop, but only two ways go anywhere.

. . . they painted a yellow stripe down the middle of Main Street, but a car came by and scattered the gravel.

. . . we used to have a bowling alley, but somebody lost the ball.

. . . when they made Main Street one way, we all left town and couldn't get back in.

. . . the only street light is the RC machine in front of the general store.

. . . the only traffic sign says, "Stop, if you've got the time."

★ ★ ★

"I hear Grandpa's gonna take a trip to Las Vegas. I wonder if there's enough excitement there for him?"
"Well, he's packing his checkerboard, just in case."

★ ★ ★

"Your town is so small, I'll bet the only activity is at the post office."
"What's a post office?"

★ ★ ★

"This is an awfully small town, isn't it?"
"No, the town's plenty big. There just ain't nearly enough people in it."

★ ★ ★

"Our town used to have a curfew law, but we repealed it."
"How come?"
"Everytime that bell rang at nine o'clock, it'd wake everybody up."

★ ★ ★

"Man, this town is really back in the sticks!"
"Naw. We're only fifteen minutes from Knoxville—by telephone."

★ ★ ★

"Do they have driver's education classes in your town?"
"They did for a while, but then the mule died."

Clothes/Clothing

When the store manager returned from lunch, he noticed his clerk's hand was bandaged, but before he could ask about the bandage, the clerk had some very good news for him.

"Guess what, sir?!" the clerk said. "I finally sold that terrible, ugly suit we've had so long!"

"Do you mean that repulsive pink-and-blue double-breasted thing?!" the manager asked.

"That's the one!"

"That's great!" the manager cried, "I thought we'd never get rid of that monstrosity! That had to be the ugliest suit we've ever had! But tell me. Why is your hand bandaged?"

"Oh," the clerk replied, "after I sold the guy that suit, his guide dog bit me."

★ ★ ★

First Woman: Did you see the sweater I knitted for Mary?
Very Buxom Second Woman: I thought you said you were making that sweater for me.
First Woman: Well, I was, but I didn't have enough yarn.

★ ★ ★

"How do you like her new bikini?"
"It reminds me of someone trying to put twenty pounds of potatoes in a ten-pound sack."

★ ★ ★

"This dress style is called a 'cutaway'."
"Yeah, and if it was any more cut away, it wouldn't have reached."

★ ★ ★

I'll have you know, this suit cost almost three hundred dollars. 'Course, it came with a used car.

★ ★ ★

Wife to Husband: I want you to explain why I have to wear these same old clothes, month after month after month?!
Husband: Because if you didn't, you'd scare the dog.

★ ★ ★

"Is that lady's dress torn, or am I seeing things?"
"Both."

★ ★ ★

"Say, what's the big idea, wearing my brand new raincoat?"
"You wouldn't want me to get your brand new shirt wet, would you?"

★ ★ ★

"I hear Francie's new dress fits her like a glove."
"That's true. She sticks out in five places."

★ ★ ★

The fellow was being sold a very cheap suit.
"But the left arm is a lot longer than the right arm," he complained.
"That's why the suit is such a bargain," the sales clerk ex-

plained. "Just cock your left shoulder up a little, like this, and tuck this left lapel under your chin a bit, like this."

"But the right leg is way too short," the customer argued.

"No problem," the sales clerk answered. "Just keep your right knee bent a little at all times, walk like this, and no one will notice. That's why this suit is only thirty dollars."

Finally, the fellow bought the suit, cocked his left shoulder into the air, tucked the suit's left lapel under his chin, bent his right knee, and limped out of the store toward his car.

Two doctors happened along and noticed him.

"Good heavens," the first doctor said to the second, "Look at that poor crippled fellow."

"Yeah," answered the second doctor. "But doesn't that suit fit great?"

Contests

"I hear your cousin got hurt when he visited your house for the weekend."

"Yeah, we were having a contest to see who could make my mother-in-law the maddest, and he won."

Cooking

"He says he'd rather kiss his wife than eat."
"I've tasted her cooking. I don't blame him."

★ ★ ★

Husband to Wife: Good grief! Don't tell me we're having spaghetti again tonight!

Wife: You liked it all right on Monday and Tuesday, and it was good enough on Wednesday and Thursday. Now, all of a sudden, on Friday you tell me you don't want spaghetti!

★ ★ ★

Wife to Husband: Don't you forget—I won a contest with my cooking.
Husband: You can't count that. It was sponsored by D-Con.

★ ★ ★

She's the only person I know who times her meals with a smoke detector.

★ ★ ★

The best way to hide something from my wife is to put it in the oven.

★ ★ ★

Wife to Husband: Wake up! I hear a rat eating last night's dinner scraps.
Husband: Go back to sleep. I'll bury it in the morning.

Cosmetics

"I just found out that peanut oil comes from peanuts, and olive oil comes from olives."
"So?"
"So I gave away all my hair oil."

Cowboys

"The name of my ranch is The Big Zero Circle K Crooked B Seven-Eleven Big Mac Bar W Double M Little J Underlined X Double Up And Go."
"Wow! I'll bet you have a lot of cattle!"
"No, they all ran off when they saw the branding iron."

★ ★ ★

"What goes 'clomp, ting-a-ling, clomp, ting-a-ling, clomp, ting-a-ling'?"
"A cowboy looking for his other spur."

★ ★ ★

"I see you're wearing only one spur."
"Yeah, I figure if one side of the horse starts running, so will the other."

★ ★ ★

A cowboy came out of the saloon to find someone had painted his horse purple. He stormed back into the saloon and picked up a barstool.

"All right," he screamed, "I want to know which one of you low-down, dirty, sidewinders painted my horse purple?!"

A huge giant of a cowboy slowly stood up, took the barstool from the cowboy, broke it over his knee, and answered, "I painted your horse purple. What have you got to say about that?"

To which the cowboy replied, "Well, I thought you might want to know it's ready for a second coat."

Crime/Criminals

"I didn't know you had a brother who used to live in Atlanta. How long did he live there?"
"Two-to-five years."

★ ★ ★

Judge to Drunken Defendant: Are you sober enough to understand you were brought here for drinking again?
Defendant: Count me out, Your Honor. I can't hold anymore.

★ ★ ★

Prosecutor to Witness: Have you ever taken a bribe to throw a court case?
Judge to Witness: Well? Answer the question!
Witness: Oh! Excuse me, Your Honor. I thought he was talkin' to you.

★ ★ ★

That man is so crooked, he has to screw on his socks.

★ ★ ★

Judge to Defendant: You're charged with driving eighty miles per hour in a twenty-mile-per-hour speed zone through the middle of town at three o'clock in the morning without your headlights on. How do you plead?
Defendant: Innocent, Your Honor! I got a good excuse.
Judge: What is it?
Defendant: The car was stolen.

★ ★ ★

"The judge fined me for stealing again."
"Why in the world do you keep stealing?"
"I have to steal to pay those fines."

★ ★ ★

Prosecutor to Judge: Your honor, due to the absence of eye-witnesses and the circumstantial nature of the evidence, plus improper search and seizure procedures by the sheriff's office, we at the prosecuting attorney's office seem to have no alternative but to dismiss the charges against the defendant.
Judge: Case dismissed!
Defendant: Your Honor, does that mean I have to give back the chickens?

★ ★ ★

"I saw a poster at the post office that says, 'Man Wanted For Car Theft.'"
"What does it pay?"

★ ★ ★

"He has to keep making moonshine because the judge took away his only other source of income."
"How did the judge do that?"
"He ordered him to quit stealing."

★ ★ ★

Judge to Defendant: These five witnesses each claim they paid you five dollars for a fruit jar full of moonshine. How do you plead?
Defendant: Innocent, Your Honor! There's no law against selling fruit jars.

★ ★ ★

"He was arrested for doing his Christmas shopping early."
"There's no crime against that."
"He was doing it before the store opened."

★ ★ ★

"I must warn you that everything you say will be held against you."
"Dolly Parton, Jesse Colter, Madonna, Crystal Gale. . . ."

★ ★ ★

Judge: The State has five eyewitnesses that say they saw you run off with that typewriter, yet you claim it was a case of mistaken identity?
Defendant: That's right, Your Honor. I thought that thing was a cash register.

★ ★ ★

"I hear your uncle went to jail for stealing."
"That's not quite right. He went to jail because he got caught stealing."

★ ★ ★

"You say you used to know a sneak thief with only one finger?"

"Yeah. The only things he could steal were doughnuts and spare tires."

★ ★ ★

"How many crooks live in this town besides you?"

"That sounds like an insult."

"Alright. How many crooks live in this town, including you?"

Dating

"Do you mean to tell me you were just going to date my girlfriend without any warning at all?!"

"What is it I should be warned about?"

★ ★ ★

Judy: I had that gorgeous man we've all been trying to date banging on my door last night for almost half an hour.

Trudy: Why didn't you open it?

Judy: I didn't want to let him out.

★ ★ ★

He: Did you know that all really great lovers are hard of hearing?

She: No, I didn't.

He: What?!

★ ★ ★

"How did your ice-skating date turn out?"

"It fell through."

★ ★ ★

"Would you consider going out with a man like me?"

"Yes . . . so long as he wasn't too much like you."

★ ★ ★

"I heard you and Sally broke up. What happened?"
"Would you date somebody who cheats and lies and flirts
with other people?"
"No, I wouldn't."
"Well, neither will Sally."

★ ★ ★

Girl: Sometimes it seems like everything I do is wrong.
Boy: Are you busy tonight?

★ ★ ★

"I feel like going out with Dolly Parton again."
"Again?"
"Yeah, I've felt like it before."

★ ★ ★

"Somebody should teach that girl right from wrong."
"All right. You teach her right, and I'll handle the rest."

★ ★ ★

First Young Woman: I've decided to throw myself at that new
   man in town.
Second Young Woman: But I heard he prefers women who
   play hard to get.
First Young Woman: Honey, I'm not playing. I mean business.

★ ★ ★

Ed: My girlfriend's father said if I could add four plus six, I
   could marry his daughter. I thought real fast and said, "Four
   plus six is eleven."
Fred: Whew! That was close!
Ed: That's the trouble. He said it was close enough.

★ ★ ★

Romeo: Say, cutie, how would you like to go to the mountains with me this weekend?
Young Woman: I don't think my mother would like that.
Romeo: No problem. We won't invite her.

★ ★ ★

"I can tell she's a girl who always gets what she goes after."
"How do you know that?"
"For one thing, she fills out her diary a week in advance."

★ ★ ★

"I'd like to find a man I can mold exactly the way I want."
"How about George?"
"No, not that moldy."

★ ★ ★

Judy: Billy got fresh with me last night, so I slapped his face. But I was sorry just as soon as I did it.
Trudy: Because you care about him?
Judy: No, because he was chewing tobacco.

Debts/Debtors

The loan company sent the fellow a letter saying, "We are surprised that we haven't received a thing as payment on your debt."

They received a reply saying, "There's no reason to be surprised. I didn't send anything."

Dentists

Yesterday, I got even with my dentist. When he got finished, I said, "This may hurt a little, Doc. I don't have any money."

"... My daughter tells me you're studying to be a dentist ..."

Diaries

"What's that you're reading?"
"A diary."
"What's in it?"
"I can't tell you that! A diary is a highly personal and confidential affair. It has important secret dreams and secret yearnings. It's private. It's not meant to be shared lightly with other people. Besides, this belongs to Mary."

Diet

Diet Quiz

If you must answer "yes" to 10 or more of these questions, you may want to consider restricting your future calorie intake.

• Has your neighborhood supermarket ever offered to send for you with a limo?

• After ordering lunch at a fast-food drive-through window, has it ever been delivered to your car on a hand truck?

• Within the last month, have you burned out more than two refrigerator bulbs?

• Do people often decide to follow you up on the next elevator?

• Has your fork ever suddenly come up missing?

• Have you ever broken out in a cold sweat when you realized you were more than a mile from the nearest Taco Bell?

• Is there a restraining order against you from the Association Of All-You-Can-Eat Restaurants?

• Have you ever spent a significant amount of time going from the first to the second floor on an escalator?

• On a recent Caribbean cruise, did the captain order you to stay in the center of the ship?

- Do your picnics in the country involve renting a U-Haul?
- Does the left side of your Pinto seem to bottom out a lot?
- Does your street always seem to have more chuckholes than other streets?

★ ★ ★

"Why is your cousin trying to lose weight again? She's already the skinniest girl in town."
"Some people are afraid of heights. She's afraid of widths."

★ ★ ★

Try my wife's new recipe for a diet dinner . . . Don't worry, you won't eat much.

★ ★ ★

"My cousin's always on one diet or another."
"Looks like she's been on several at once."

Diplomacy

Man at Bar to Bartender: I don't know why, but I've always found it difficult to make friends. Know what I mean, Bozonose?

★ ★ ★

Diplomacy is something you learn after you're too old for it to do you any good.

Directions

"Am I on the right road to the Grand Ole Opry?"
"I don't know. Can you sing through your nose?"

★ ★ ★

"Does this road lead to St. Louis?"
"It does about half the time. Depends which way you go."

★ ★ ★

"Could you tell me how to get to McMinnville from here?"
"Sure. Go up here three miles and turn left on Jackson Road
. . . wait, that won't work. Go on back there four miles and
take a right on Old Smith Road . . . no, wait, that won't work,
either. Hmm. To tell you the truth, mister, if I was going to
McMinnville, I wouldn't start from here at all."

★ ★ ★

"Are there any good girls in this town?"
"Mister, all the girls in this town are good girls."
"Then how far is it to the next town?"

Divorce

Alimony is a contraction. It's short for "all my money."

★ ★ ★

"Did the judge split everything fairly when he granted your
wife a divorce?"
"Sort of. She got to keep the house, the car, the boat, the
furniture, and the dog. I got to keep everything I was wearing."

★ ★ ★

She's had so many divorces, she's spent more time in court
than Perry Mason.

★ ★ ★

He left his wife for a good reason. She divorced him.

★ ★ ★

"His wife is suing him for divorce."
"How come?"
"Incompatibility."
"How in the world did she catch him doing that?"

★ ★ ★

"She's anxious to get a new husband."
"New husband? I didn't know she was divorced."
"She's not."

★ ★ ★

"You look like my fifth husband."
"Your fifth husband? How many husbands have you had?"
"Four."

★ ★ ★

The lawyer seemed confident he could win a good divorce settlement for his female client.

"Don't worry about a thing," he told her. "We'll convince the judge that your husband mesmerized you into marrying him with his charming, delightful personality and his handsome, little boy smile. He overwhelmed you with his sparkling, upbeat personality. He beguiled you with his insightful conversation and towering intellect. He swept you off your feet with his masterful lovemaking techniques and attentive behavior . . ."

"Hold it, hold it!" the woman cried. "If that creep is as good as all that, I've changed my mind."

★ ★ ★

"It seems like common sense would prevent a lot of divorces."
"Yes. And a lot of marriages."

★ ★ ★

★ ★ ★

Woman's Letter to Ex-husband:

Dear Charlie,
    I'm writing to say that I realize our divorce was entirely my fault. I still love you. I want you to know that if I ever get the chance, I would make it all up to you by being the most perfect wife you could ever hope to have. I finally realize how wonderful you are and how stupid I was to lose you.
(Signed) Beverly
P.S. Congratulations on winning the lottery.

Doctors

Doctor to Patient: I see you're over a month late for your appointment. Don't you know that nervous disorders require prompt and regular attention? What's your excuse?
Patient: I was just following your orders, Doc.
Doctor: Following my orders? What are you talking about? I gave you no such order.
Patient: You told me to avoid people who irritate me.

★ ★ ★

Doctor to Patient: I'll have you know I've been practicing medicine over ten years.
Patient: Call me when you're done practicing and decide to get serious.

★ ★ ★

An old man strode into his doctor's office and said, "Doc, my druggist said to tell you to change my prescription and to check the prescription you've been givin' to Mrs. Wilcox."

"Oh, he did, did he?" the doctor shot back. "And since when does a druggist second-guess a doctor's advice?"

"Since he found out I've been on birth control pills since February."

★ ★ ★

"Doc, my neighbor's been drinking something called 'Magic Youth Potion,' and he looks better every day.

"He's being swindled, you fool. How much has he spent on that crap?"

"Quite a bit. He's been drinking it for a hundred twelve years."

★ ★ ★

Doctor: Mrs. Smith, I have to tell you, I don't like the looks of your husband.
Patient's Wife: Neither do I, but he's good to the children.

★ ★ ★

Patient to Doctor: I'm terribly nervous, doctor. This is my very first trip to an operating room.
Doctor: I know what you mean. It's mine, too.

★ ★ ★

The ninety-year-old man told the doctor he was concerned about his love life slowing down.

"When did you first notice it?" the doctor asked.

"Well, Doc," the old man answered, "twice last night and again this morning."

★ ★ ★

The ninety-year-old man was in for his checkup when the doctor learned he was about to marry an eighteen-year-old girl.

"Now, Mr. Jenkins," the doctor warned, "you should know that when a man your age marries an eighteen-year-old girl, somebody could get hurt."

The old man shrugged, "If she dies, she dies."

★ ★ ★

"How are you feeling since your operation?"

"A lot better. Doctor says, in a couple of weeks I'll be strong enough to look at his bill."

★ ★ ★

Doctor to Elderly Patient: Mr. Smith, that last check you gave me came back.
Patient: Then we're even, Doc. So did my arthritis.

★ ★ ★

"Doc, do you have anything that will cure fleas?"
"Maybe. What made them sick?"

★ ★ ★

"The doctor said I was suffering from depression. He said, if he was me, he'd go home and take his wife out for dinner and a few drinks."
"Are you going to do it?"
"Yeah, I'm picking his wife up at six-thirty."

★ ★ ★

"Doc, that medicine you gave me was marked 'For Adults Only,' right?"
"That's right."
"But I ain't got the Adults; I got the flu."

★ ★ ★

"The doctor says I've got an itchy ulna."
"I thought you drove an American car."

★ ★ ★

"You look like something's bothering you."
"Yeah, all the plants in my doctor's waiting room are dead."

★ ★ ★

"Did you hear about Dr. Jones fighting with his girlfriend?"
"No, I didn't."
"They got to yelling at one another, and he told her she was a lousy kisser."
"Oh-oh. What did she do then?"
"She decided to get a second opinion."

Drunks/Drinking

"Why do you suppose Old Man Barkley drinks so much?"
"He drinks so much because he worries so much."
"What's he worried about?"
"He's worried about drinking so much."

★ ★ ★

"I had a bad cold, and a fellow told me the best thing for it was to drink a quart of whiskey and go home to bed. . . . On the way home, another fellow told me the same thing. That made a half-gallon."

—Mark Twain

★ ★ ★

There's a new drink made with vodka and carrot juice. You get just as drunk, but you can see better in the morning.

★ ★ ★

She: Is it true, you were fired from your job for attending your uncle's funeral?
He: Yeah, my boss said three days was too long to take off work for a funeral.
She: Three days?! Why did you need three days off work?
He: My uncle was a big drinker, and he gave orders to be cremated. It took us three days to put out the flames.

★ ★ ★

"I saw your husband at the amusement park, and he'd been drinking again."
"How could you tell?"
"He got off the roller coaster, staggering and dizzy and sick, and said to the fellow next to him, 'Something tells me I took the wrong bus.'"

★ ★ ★

The traffic cop spotted a drunken driver weaving and speeding and finally forced him to pull over.

"What's the big idea, driving like an idiot?" the cop demanded.

"I can't help it," the drunk replied. "I'm sick."

"Sick, huh? And what about those empty beer cans all over the seat beside you? You've been drinking all day long, haven't you."

"That's right, officer," the drunk answered. "And don't try to tell me that ain't a sickness."

★ ★ ★

First Drunk: Is that sun setting, or is it rising?
Second Drunk: I don't know. I don't even live around here.

★ ★ ★

A drunk came from a bar at two o'clock in the morning and promptly walked into the nearest light post. Unable to see well, he felt the post carefully with his hands and proceeded to walk all around it three or four times, examining all sides of the post with his hands. Finally, he slumped down on the curb and buried his head in his hands.

"It's no use," he sobbed. "I'm walled in."

★ ★ ★

"Her first husband drowned in a big vat of beer."

"Oooo! That must have been horrible for him!"

"Well, it couldn't have been all that bad. He got out twice for pretzels."

★ ★ ★

"They say that drinking is bad for you, but I can definitely testify that drinking makes my wife more beautiful."

"Wait a minute. I didn't know your wife drank?"

"She doesn't. I do."

Electricity

My aunt Martha was electrocuted when the hair dryer shorted out. Now, every year we hang a wreath on the fusebox.

Employees

The pretty young secretary was bragging to her girlfriend, "My boss gave me a full-length mink coat for my birthday."

"Whoa!" her friend replied. "What in the world did you have to do for it?"

"Not much, just shorten the sleeves a bit."

★ ★ ★

"His wife fired his beautiful new secretary less than a week after he hired her."

"Didn't she want to give her a chance?"

"No, she didn't want to give *him* a chance."

★ ★ ★

"I get the feeling I'm going to get my old boss back again."

"I thought your old boss died?"

"He did die—and the company's going to the same place he did."

★ ★ ★

Young Man to Office Manager: I've come to take the job you advertised in the paper.

Manager: Oh, you have, have you? What are your qualifications?

Young Man: Well, I graduated from Harvard with the highest grade in history. I sold over a million magazines before I graduated high school. In my class at Yale, I was voted Most Likely To Succeed and Best Liked, and I was the youngest man in history to write a best-selling book about Business Management.

Manager: My goodness! That's wonderful! Do you have any bad points at all?

Young Man: Just one . . . I'm a pathological liar.

★ ★ ★

"How many employees work in your factory?"
"Oh, I'd say about half of them."

★ ★ ★

"I hear your boss is mean."
"Let's just say he knows Saddam Hussein's home phone number."

★ ★ ★

"Would you hire someone like me?"
"Sure . . . as long as they weren't too much like you."

★ ★ ★

"If I hire you for this job, do you think you can keep busy?"
"Well, just in case, I'll bring some crossword puzzles."

★ ★ ★

Employer to Inventory Clerk: Why in the world did you order five thousand bottles of aspirin?!

Inventory Clerk: Because we're out of cotton balls.

★ ★ ★

Employer to New Cashier: Honesty is very important when you're in charge of the cash register. Let's say a customer buys something for five dollars, but gives you a ten-dollar bill by mistake. What do you do?

Cashier: Hmmm . . . I guess I'd have to decide whether or not to split it with you.

★ ★ ★

Employer to Tardy Employee: I hope you have a very good reason for being late for work!
Employee: Of course, I do, sir! You don't think I'd be late for work without having a good reason, do you?
Employer: Well, what is it?
Employee: It makes the day seem a lot shorter.

★ ★ ★

"I'd like to apply for the job as secretary."
"Can you write in shorthand?"
"Oh, sure . . . but it takes a lot longer."

★ ★ ★

"Why did you quit your job at the toll booth?"
"Because my mother always told me, 'Never take money from strangers.' "

★ ★ ★

"On your job application, you say you used to be a professional 'moanback'? What, exactly, does a professional moanback do?"
"He's the guy on back of the trash truck who keeps yelling, 'Moan back! Moan back!' "

★ ★ ★

"He claims he used to be a professional pilot."
"Yeah, his brothers would cut wood and he'd pile it."

★ ★ ★

"I am not going back to work until my boss takes back what he said to me."
"What did he say?"
"He said, 'You're fired.' "

★ ★ ★

The warehouse foreman walked up on the stock man and caught him loafing.

"Hey!" the foreman shouted. "Why aren't you working?"
"Because I didn't see you coming."

★ ★ ★

The fellow was applying for the job as night watchman and was asked why he felt he was qualified for the job.
"Well, for one thing," he answered, "I'm a real light sleeper."

★ ★ ★

The pretty young secretary had been transferred to the company's Dallas office.
"We operate the same here in Dallas as you did in Detroit," her supervisor told her.
"Alright then," she answered. "Kiss me so we can get started."

Engagements

"I heard you're engaged to a girl in Centertown."
"Yep, that's right."
"But you told me you were engaged to a girl in Springfield."
"That's right, too."
"How can you be engaged to two different girls in two different towns?"
"I've got a bicycle."

Escalators

"I hear she was at a department store when the power failed."
"Yeah. . . . She was trapped on the escalator for forty-five minutes."

Etiquette

She thinks good manners is putting cream in your coffee before you pour it in your saucer.

★ ★ ★

For years, we thought the neighbor boy had freckles. Turned out, his folks were teaching him to eat with a fork.

Evolution

"All this talk about evolution. I can't see what difference it makes to me if one of my grandfathers was a monkey."

"Maybe not, but I'll bet it made a big difference to one of your grandmothers."

Exercise

"I wonder why people sweat when they exercise?"
"So they won't catch fire."

★ ★ ★

"I hear exercise kills germs."
"That's silly. How do you get a germ to exercise?"

★ ★ ★

"I hear your wife's got you on a strict exercise program. Do you feel like a new man?"
"I sure do. The old one wasn't so sore."

Faces

"I could swear I've seen your face somewhere else."
"No, it's always been right here on front of my head."

★ ★ ★

"I can pick a face out of a crowd just like that!"
"Then why in the world did you pick that one?"

Failure/Failures

"I've decided I'm not the biggest failure in my family."
"You're not?"
"No, I've decided that my father is the biggest failure in my family."
"Why's that?"
"He spent his whole life trying to make me amount to somethin'."

False Teeth

"My mother-in-law just bought her twelfth set of false teeth."
"Good heavens! Does she lose them or break them?"
"Neither. She wears them out."

Family

"Sir, your daughter says she loves me, and she can't live without me, and she wants to marry me."
"And you're asking my permission to marry her?"
"No, I'm asking you to make her leave me alone."

★ ★ ★

"Why in the world did your parents name your little brother
'Encore'?"
"Because he wasn't on their program."

★ ★ ★

"I hear the Martins took their thirteen children to the parade."
"With thirteen children, they *were* the parade."

★ ★ ★

"What did your parents want you to do when you grew up?"
"Leave home."

★ ★ ★

The first half of your life is dominated by your parents; the
second half is dominated by your children.

★ ★ ★

"They say unhappiness is a relative matter."
"I know mine is."

★ ★ ★

He's got a good enough family tree; it's the crop that failed.

★ ★ ★

"How many brothers and sisters do you have?"
"Three."
"Are you the oldest in your family?"
"No, silly. Daddy is."

★ ★ ★

He's her second cousin. The first one resigned.

★ ★ ★

Father to Daughter: It's a good thing you chose to take accounting at school.
Daughter: How come?
Father: Because I want you to account for coming home at five A.M. this morning.

★ ★ ★

Father to Daughter's Suitor: So you want to marry my daughter, huh? You should know, I've had a hard time keeping that girl in clothes.
Suitor: Yes, sir, she's that same way with me.

★ ★ ★

Father to Daughter: Do you have a good excuse for coming home at three o'clock in the morning?
Daughter: Yes, I do, Father. The party was raided.

★ ★ ★

"Daddy, Charlie asked me to marry him, but I told him I couldn't leave Mama."
"Oh, that's okay. Take her with you."

★ ★ ★

My family's business was wiped out when they invented automatic car washes.

★ ★ ★

"I had so many brothers and sisters, Mom used to count noses before every meal. And the way we ate, Dad used to count noses *after* every meal."

★ ★ ★

Daughter to Father: Daddy, do you think somebody should be punished for something they didn't do?
Father: Of course not, honey.
Daughter: That's a relief! I didn't come home last night.

★ ★ ★

"Every week, I send my mother a check."
"What a wonderful thing to do! What does she do with it?"
"She signs it and sends it back."

★ ★ ★

My parents had so many kids, the county decided to just go ahead and build the new school next door.

★ ★ ★

"Have you ever had your family's ancestors traced?"
"I had an uncle traced to Canada once."

★ ★ ★

Mother told me to have a good time at the party, and to be a good girl. I just wish she'd make up her mind.

★ ★ ★

I grew up on the tenth floor of a high rise apartment building. Mom used to send me and my brother out on the balcony to play with Frisbees.

★ ★ ★

"Did you hear that Charlie Renfro thinks he might be related to you?"
"Never mind him. Charlie's an idiot."
"Yes, but that might be just a coincidence."

★ ★ ★

The little boy decided to run away from home, but since he wasn't allowed to cross the street, he didn't get very far. After about three hours, he went back home, but no one even knew he'd been gone.

He wandered around the house for a few minutes, then finally asked his mother, "Is that the same dog we had before I went away?"

★ ★ ★

When we held my brother one way, he looked like mother; and when we held him another way, he looked like father. But we couldn't make him look like father too long at once; the blood would rush to his head.

Famous Last Words Department

- Let's see if it's loaded.
- Gimme a match. I think the pilot light is out.
- We can make it easy. I don't even see a train.
- If you knew anything at all, you wouldn't be a traffic cop.
- What's this red button?
- Don't worry; my husband won't be home for hours.

Farming/Farmers

At supper, the farmer announced to his family that he intended to spend the next day spreading manure on the fields.

"Daddy," his daughter replied, "I wish you'd use the word *fertilizer* instead of *manure*."

"Don't complain, sweetheart," the farmer's wife said. "It took me five years to get him to use the word *manure*."

★ ★ ★

"These melons you're selling for a dollar and a half apiece, did you raise them yourself?"

"Yep. Yesterday, they were a dollar and a quarter."

★ ★ ★

"My mule won't plow anymore, and my cows won't give as much milk as they used to."

"Sounds like you and that ole mule are both losing your pull."

★ ★ ★

"Do you think the government should make it easier for the average farmer to borrow money?"

"Not necessarily, but I think they should make it easier for him to pay it back."

★ ★ ★

"You're not going to milk the cows in that pretty dress, are you?"

"No, silly, in this bucket."

★ ★ ★

"My new boyfriend is a truck farmer."

"Don't be silly. Trucks come from factories."

★ ★ ★

"I've been farming over ten years. There is absolutely nothing on a farm that I don't know how to do."

"Can I watch you lay an egg?"

★ ★ ★

That hen lays eggs so big, it only takes eight of them to make a dozen.

★ ★ ★

That watermelon vine grew so fast it ruined the melons dragging them across the field.

★ ★ ★

"Why did you choose to raise livestock, rather than grow crops?"

"Because livestock don't need hoein'."

★ ★ ★

"Can you tell me how long cows should be milked?"

"About the same as short ones."

★ ★ ★

"I love being a farmer. Last fall I bought a pig for thirty dollars, then I spent twenty dollars feeding him 'til spring, then I sold him for fifty dollars."

"Why, you didn't make a thing off that pig."

"No, but I had the pleasure of his company all winter."

★ ★ ★

"Last summer, we raised strawberries as big as golf balls."

"Did you put a lot of fertilizer on them?"

"Shoot, no. Milk and sugar."

★ ★ ★

The young agricultural student thought he'd learned all about farming at the state university.

"You should be irrigating that field there," he told the old farmer. "I'd be surprised if you make anything at all off the oats in that field."

"So would I," said the old farmer. "That's barley."

★ ★ ★

"Which is correct: Is a hen 'setting' or is a hen 'sitting'?"

"That doesn't matter. What's important is, is she 'laying' or 'lying'?"

★ ★ ★

"Does that cow give milk?"

"No, you got to get in there and take it."

★ ★ ★

"I hear your crops weren't too good this year."

"Nope. Last night for supper, we had a half-acre of corn."

★ ★ ★

He forgot to turn off his daddy's new milking machine and turned all the cows inside out.

★ ★ ★

The farmer made a practice of loading his three cows in the wagon at dawn every Friday morning to let them visit with the neighbor's bull.

Finally, the neighbor sold the bull, and about noon that next Friday, the farmer happened to look out the window. Two of those cows were in the wagon, and the third one was hitching up the mule.

★ ★ ★

"Is it all right if I pay you five dollars for that hen I just ran over?"

"Better make it ten. That was my rooster's only hen, and the shock might kill him, too."

★ ★ ★

"Doesn't the smell of raising pigs ever bother you?"
"Depends on the price of pork."

★ ★ ★

"Was your farm hurt by that tornado?"
"Nope. I got a tool shed and six hogs more than I had before."

★ ★ ★

The visitor couldn't help but notice the pigs dozing in the farmer's living room. He couldn't contain himself.

"It's not healthy to let pigs sleep in your house," he said.

"Phooey," was the farmer's reply. "We ain't lost a pig in years."

★ ★ ★

"In the old days, where did they keep milk so it wouldn't sour?"
"In the cow."

★ ★ ★

"No fresh milk today?"
"No. Our new calf got in the barn and drank it all up."
"How did it get the lids off the bottles?"

★ ★ ★

"I used to quit plowing for lunch everyday at exactly eleven-thirty."
"Did you have a wristwatch or a pocket watch?"
"Neither. The whistle down at the sawmill blows everyday at noon, and I'd just quit a half-hour before I heard it."

★ ★ ★

"Charlie Johnson moved back into town."
"But I thought Charlie was a farmer."
"That's exactly the same mistake he made."

Feet

"My feet were so cold, I couldn't sleep last night."
"Why didn't you use a hot water bottle?"
"I tried, but I couldn't get either foot through that little hole."

★ ★ ★

His feet are so big, he has to put his pants on over his head.

Fighting

Judge to Defendant: Did you, or did you not, hit the plaintiff on the veranda?
Defendant: No, sir, Your Honor. I hit him on top the head.

★ ★ ★

"I hear you lost a fight last night."
"Yeah, he hit me so hard, my socks changed feet."

★ ★ ★

"There were only two hits when he and I fought. He hit me, and I hit the ground."

★ ★ ★

"What's that?"
"This is a list of people I can whip."
"Oh, it is, is it? And I see my name is right up there near the top!"
"Yep."
"Why, you miserable wimp! I could whip you with one hand tied behind my back!"
"You think so?"
"Yes! I could stand you upside down and pound you in the ground like a tent stake!"
"Are you sure about that?"
"I've never been more sure of anything in my entire life!"
"Okay. In that case, I'd better erase your name from the list."

★ ★ ★

First Man: What happened to you?
Second Man: Fred beat me up.
First Man: What? Why, you were bragging all over town just yesterday how you could whip Fred, hands down!
Second Man: Yeah, but he didn't keep his hands down.

★ ★ ★

"Don't start a fight with me. I'm the kind of guy that'll cut and shoot."
"You?! Cut and shoot?!"
"Uh-huh. I'll cut down the alley and shoot around the corner."

★ ★ ★

"I hear you were there when that big brawl broke out last night."
"I sure was. I was right in the middle of it."
"Did you get hurt in the fracas?"
"No, but I got hurt everyplace else."

Fire/Fire Department

"Cletus said that when the fire broke out at the motel, he led everyone to safety."
"You might say that. He was the first one out."

A woman called the fire department and reported a burglar was trying to get through her bedroom window.
"Lady, this is the fire department," answered the dispatcher. "You want the police department."
"No, I don't," said the lady. "My bedroom's on the second floor, and he needs a longer ladder."

Fish/Fishing

A fish net is nothing but a lot of little holes tied together.

"I hear you've been bragging about a fish you caught yesterday."
"I sure have! That fish was so big, the photograph weighed six pounds."

Floods

Floodwaters forced a preacher to the second story of his house. A fireman came along in a motorboat and said, "Get in.

The water's still rising."

"No, thanks," the preacher answered. "I'd rather stay. The Lord will protect me."

The fireman left, and the waters rose until the fellow was forced to his attic.

A National Guardsman came along in another boat and called, "Hop in! It's still raining upstream!"

The believer again declined. "No. The Lord will protect me."

The Guardsman left, and the waters rose and forced the fellow out on his roof to cling to his chimney.

A helicopter came, and the pilot dropped a rope ladder and called over his loudspeaker, "Climb up the ladder!"

But the man still declined, convinced that the Lord would protect him.

The helicopter left, and the fellow drowned.

At heaven's gate, he said to Saint Peter, "What's going on here? I put my faith in the Lord to protect me, but I still drowned!"

"Don't blame the Lord," Saint Peter replied. "He sent you two boats and a helicopter."

Food

"Did this cheese come from Switzerland?"
"Yes."
"Was it *im*ported or *de*ported?"

★ ★ ★

"I hate this cheese with the holes in it."
"Then eat around 'em."

Fools

They say a fool and his money are soon parted, but how did a fool get that money in the first place?

★ ★ ★

"I guess y'all came to hear the latest dope from the country . . . here I am."

★ ★ ★

"He's so dumb, he traded his only horse for a bale of hay."
"What does he intend to do with the hay?"
"He's gonna see if he can borrow back the horse long enough to get rid of it."

Football

"When you were on the football team, what position did you play?"
"Bent over like this . . ."

★ ★ ★

Two fellows had been together in hell for several years, shoveling coal into the fires side by side. To their astonishment, they suddenly felt cold air.

The air got colder and colder. It began to snow; then the snow became a blizzard. The fires were extinguished by a covering of snow, and an icy blast of wind swept over everything.

"Brrr! What's going on?" the first fellow asked in amazement.

"I'm just guessing," the other said, shivering, "but something tells me the Colts have won the Super Bowl."

★ ★ ★

"He said that when he played college football, he was known as 'Touchdown Smith'."
"Right. One touch and down he went."

★ ★ ★

"The coach says I'm a triple threat."
"Yeah, he's never sure whether you're going to fumble, run the wrong way, or jump offside."

★ ★ ★

"I remember our whole football team was scared to death to play against the state champions. Even before the game started, the score was zero-to-zero in their favor."

★ ★ ★

"That was the roughest football game I was ever in. Saddam Hussein was in the stands, and he had to cover his eyes."

★ ★ ★

"When I told the football coach that George would make a good player, the coach told me George would need three things:
"'He'll need dedication,' the coach said, and I said, 'Coach, George has plenty of dedication.'
"He said, 'He'll need stamina,' and I said, 'He's got plenty of stamina.'
"He said, 'He'll need intelligence,' and I said, 'He's got his own football shoes.'"

★ ★ ★

"I hear George was the hero of the day at last Sunday's football game."
"Yeah, he had his uniform on backwards, and the other team thought he was running the wrong way."

Funrals

A distraught man was seated on the steps outside a funeral home, weeping and sobbing, when another fellow happened along and asked him why he was weeping.

"My wife died two days ago," the man answered, "and I can't bear the thought of sleeping alone!"

"But things change," the second man said, trying to comfort him. "In a few months, there's a good chance you'll meet another fine lady and fall in love all over again."

"Maybe so," sobbed the first man, "but what about tonight?"

★ ★ ★

First Spinster: I see in the paper where Annie Walker just had her third husband cremated.

Second Spinster: I know. Some of us can't get a husband; others have husbands to burn.

★ ★ ★

The fellow was dying at home in bed when he called in his wife from the kitchen and told her, "I think my time has come, darling, but I can smell your wonderful apple pies cooking, and I'd like one more piece before I die."

"Oh, I'm sorry, dear," his wife answered. "Those are for the family after the funeral."

★ ★ ★

A fellow died while he and his wife were vacationing in Arizona. He was brought back east for a funeral in his hometown.

At the funeral, a friend viewed the body and commented to the dead man's wife: "He certainly looks wonderful."

"Yes," the wife answered, "those two weeks in Arizona did him a world of good."

★ ★ ★

Wife to Husband: If I die, I want you to promise me, in the funeral procession, you'll let my mother ride in the first car with you.

Husband: All right, but it'll ruin my day.

★ ★ ★

The husband was going through the monthly bills.

"For Pete's sake," he exclaimed to his wife, "here's another bill from the funeral parlor for another fifteen dollars! What's this all about?"

"That's more of the bill for Uncle Fred's funeral," his wife answered.

"Baloney. Your Uncle Fred was buried over eight months ago. How can they still be billing us?"

"Well, you remember poor Uncle Fred didn't have a dark blue suit, so I rented one."

Gambling

A fellow was about to enter a bar when a dog said to him, "Hey, mister! Wanna make some quick money?"

The man couldn't believe his ears. He said to the dog, "Can you talk?"

"Yeah," the dog answered, "and that's how we can pick up some easy money. You take me into the bar with you, pretend I'm your dog, and bet everybody I can talk."

The fellow thought that was a great idea, so he took the dog into the bar, set it on the bar, and announced to everyone that the dog could talk.

The other patrons didn't believe him, and it wasn't long before several thousand dollars had been bet.

Finally, after all the bets had been placed, the guy said to the dog, "All right, go ahead and say something."

Nothing.

He told the dog again, "Hey! All the bets are placed! Say something!"

The dog just looked at him and whined.

The man asked again and again, but the dog wouldn't say a word. Finally, the guy had to pay all the bets, scooped up the dog in disgust and walked out.

Once outside, he screamed, "You just cost me way over a thousand dollars! You got anything to say before I kill you?"

"Use your head, mister," the dog answered. "Tomorrow night, we'll be able to get five-to-one."

★ ★ ★

A horse stepped up to the twenty-dollar window and said, "I want to bet twenty dollars on myself to win the sixth race."

"What? I must be hearing things," the astonished clerk answered.

"I know, I know," said the horse. "You're surprised to hear a horse talk."

"No, it's not that," the guy replied. "I just don't think you've got a snowball's chance in July of winning that sixth race."

★ ★ ★

"Does your husband play cards for money?"
"No, but the men he plays against do."

★ ★ ★

It's not a good idea to gamble against a bad loser, but it beats gambling against any kind of winner.

★ ★ ★

Everybody knows you can't win if you gamble, but where does all that money go?

★ ★ ★

"I know for a fact he cheats at cards."
"How can you be so sure?"
"Last night he had four aces, but I only dealt him two."

★ ★ ★

She: Do you win at gambling?
He: Oh, you know how it is . . . I win one day, lose the next.
She: Gee, why don't you gamble every other day?

★ ★ ★

"Do you mean you had a straight flush and you didn't take the pot?"
"That's right."

"But what beats a straight flush?"
"A pair of threes and a twelve-gauge shotgun."

★ ★ ★

Judge to Defendant: You're in my court charged with gambling . . . say, haven't I seen you before?
Defendant: Sure, Your Honor. I'm your bookie.

★ ★ ★

"Grandma used to sit at the spinning wheel for hours."
"Did she enjoy making yarn?"
"No, she enjoyed playing roulette."

★ ★ ★

"My tout hasn't had a winning week in almost two months."
"Why don't you try a different tout?"
"Oh, I don't want to make him mad at me. He might stop selling me his picks."

★ ★ ★

"I'm going to the horse races, and I sure hope I break even."
"Break even? How come?"
"I need the money."

★ ★ ★

"If you could live your life over, would you change anything?"
"Yes. I wouldn't gamble."
"Did you lose a lot of money?"
"No, I made a lot of money, but I used it to get married."

★ ★ ★

"He always seems to win at cards and lose at horses."
"That's because they won't let him shuffle the horses."

★ ★ ★

"... Who dealt this mess?"

"I learned that if you give to the poor, whatever you give will come back to you tenfold."

"How'd you learn that?"

"I saw a poor-looking fellow on the street, and I gave him ten dollars and said, 'Good luck, friend.' The next day, he gave me one hundred dollars back."

"He did?"

"Yep. Good Luck Friend came in first and paid nine-to-one."

★ ★ ★

"How did you like your vacation in Las Vegas?"

"Terrible. I left my glasses at home."

"Oh-oh. Did you have trouble seeing the shows?"

"No, but I spent the first morning playing a stamp machine."

★ ★ ★

"I can't go with you this afternoon. Tonight's my father's weekly card game, so I have to stay home."

"But why do you have to stay home this afternoon because of that?"

"Because it's my turn to mark the cards."

★ ★ ★

Since Uncle Fred died, they miss him down at the horseracing track. They still leave a light burning for him in the two-dollar window.

Garbage

"I hear your brother got a job as garbage collector. Does he like it?"

"Oh, he liked it alright for the first few days, but then his head cold cleared up."

Golf

The duffer muffed his tee shot into the woods, then hit into a few trees, then proceeded to hit across the fairway into another woods. Finally, after banging away several more times, he proceeded to hit into a sand trap.

All the while, he'd noticed that the club professional had been watching.

"What club should I use now?" he asked the pro.

"I don't know," the pro replied. "What game are you playing?"

★ ★ ★

Priest to Caddy: I wonder if it would help my golf score if I prayed before I teed off?

Caddy: Only if you keep your head down, Father.

★ ★ ★

"Do you have any idea how I could cut ten or twelve strokes off my game?"

"Yeah, quit on seventeen."

★ ★ ★

A golfer sliced his tee shot into the woods and decided to try to blast out rather than take a penalty shot. His second shot went straight into a big tree trunk and bounced straight back at him. It hit him right between the eyes and killed him instantly.

Next thing he knew, he was at the Pearly Gates, and Saint Peter was trying to find his name on a list.

"Well, here's your name," Saint Peter said finally, "but it says that you're not due to die for another twenty years. How did you get here anyway?"

"In two," the golfer replied.

★ ★ ★

The golfer sliced his drive so badly off the third tee that it sailed onto the fifth fairway, hit another golfer on the head, and killed him instantly.

"This is terrible!" his partner cried. "What should we do?!"

"Well," the first golfer replied, "I think I'll try bringing my left hand over and keeping my elbow locked."

Gossip

I don't know her well enough to speak to, but I do know her well enough to talk about.

★ ★ ★

"I heard that you can't keep a secret."

"I most certainly can too! But the people I tell them to can't."

Government

During a terrible snowstorm one winter, many of the highway signs were totally covered with snow. The following spring, the state decided to raise all the signs twelve inches.

At a cost of six million dollars, each sign was equipped with a new pole, one foot longer than the old pole.

"That's an outrageous price," said a local farmer, "but I guess we're lucky the state government handled it, instead of the federal government."

"Why's that?" his neighbor asked.

"Because," the farmer answered, "knowin' the federal government, they'd have decided to lower all the highways."

Greeting Cards

"I'd like a very special greeting card, expressing my deepest love, affection, loyalty, and sincere feelings for a very special young woman."

"How about this one?"

"That's good enough. Gimme a dozen."

Groceries

Why do hot dogs come in packages of ten and hot dog buns come in packages of eight?

★ ★ ★

Wife to Husband: Have you looked in our cupboards? There's eighteen jugs of whiskey and two loaves of bread!
Husband: What are you going to do with all that bread?

Hair

"She says, with her new haircut, she doesn't look like an old lady anymore."
"She's right. She looks like an old man."

★ ★ ★

Are you wearing a new hairstyle, or are we having an electrical storm?

★ ★ ★

"I was walking along the beach with your new girlfriend the other day, and the wind blew her hair in her face."
"Oh?"
"Yes, then the wind blew her hair in my face."
"Yes, so what?"
"Well, then the wind blew her hair in the ocean."

Hearing Aids

"This new hearing aid is the best hearing aid there ever was! I couldn't hear this good even when I was a kid! I've never heard this good!"
"What kind is it?"
"A quarter 'til five."

★ ★ ★

I went to a doctor in Tennessee to have my hearing checked. He put me on the examination table, sat down next to my left ear, and told the nurse to give him his instrument. She handed him a banjo.

Heaven/Hell

"I wonder what our ancestors would think of our country today?"
"When I get to heaven, I'll ask them."
"What if they didn't go to heaven?"
"Then you ask them."

"Hee-Haw"

I like to watch "Hee-Haw" for lots of reasons. One reason is, I like those Hee-Haw Honeys. I forget the other reasons.

Hillbillies

First Hillbilly: Was that your pickup truck I saw broke down alongside the highway?
Second Hillbilly: Yep, it sure was.
First Hillbilly: Why were those roses sittin' on the hood and them one-eyed susans sittin' on the tailgate?
Second Hillbilly: Don't you know, when your truck breaks down, the law says you got to set out flares?

★ ★ ★

He lives so far back in the country, he has to go toward town to hunt.

★ ★ ★

"Grandpa, tell us again about the first time you saw an automobile."

"Well, I was just a boy, sittin' on the porch with your great-great grandaddy, when this thing came clangin' and bangin' up the road. Your great-great grandaddy grabbed up his rifle and up and took a shot at it. The driver jumped out and went runnin' off through the woods, but the automobile just kept goin'. Your great-great grandmammy was watchin', and she said, 'You didn't kill it, Luther, but you sure made it turn that fella loose!"

★ ★ ★

"That last batch o' moonshine you made was too strong."

"Couldn't you drink it?"

"Oh, I finally drank it. But now, everytime I sneeze, I burn holes in the curtains."

★ ★ ★

"Jeb went sneakin' over to see Annabelle, and Annabelle's daddy took a shot at him."

"Hit him?"

"Nope, but Jeb said that bullet came so close to his ear he heard it twice."

"Twice?"

"Yep. Once when it passed him, and once when he passed it."

Hitchhikers

The driver pulled over and asked the hitchhiker, "Are you a Republican or a Democrat?"

"What difference does that make?" the hitchhiker asked.

"Because I only give rides to Democrats," the driver answered.

"In that case," the hitchhiker said, "I'm a Democrat."

So the driver motioned the hitchhiker in and off they went.

Several miles down the road, the driver saw a field of ripe watermelons and stopped the car.

"I'll keep the car running," he said, "and you go steal us a watermelon."

"Shouldn't we just stop at some market and buy a watermelon?" the hitchhiker asked.

"Look," said the driver, "I gave you a ride. The least you can do is grab us one of those watermelons. Otherwise, find another ride."

So the hitchhiker got out, took a watermelon, got back in, and off they drove.

After they'd driven a mile, the hitchhiker began chuckling to himself, and the driver was curious.

"What are you laughing about?" the driver asked.

"Well, it just occurred to me," the hitchhiker answered, "I've only been a Democrat for ten minutes, and already I'm a thief."

Hoboes

The wealthy lady spotted the hobo on the street and gave him a quarter as she asked, "You poor man, how did you get to be so destitute?"

"I was a lot like you, lady," the hobo answered. "Squandering vast quantities of money on poor people."

★ ★ ★

The wealthy elderly lady was disgusted by the sight of the ragged hobo. "You filthy man," she said. "Don't you even have a handkerchief?"

"Yeah, I do, lady," the hobo replied. "But I don't like loanin' it out."

Holidays

Wife to Husband: I'm not spending another holiday with you in this house! Last Thanksgiving you got drunk and pitched the turkey out the window. On Christmas you almost electrocuted Mama with the tree lights. On Easter you stomped my new twenty-dollar hat. And on the Fourth of July you tried to drop a firecracker down my sister's stretchpants!

Husband: Now, you listen to me, woman. What's this world coming to if a man can't celebrate a holiday?

★ ★ ★

A toast: May all your troubles last as long as your New Year's resolutions.

★ ★ ★

Santa Claus reminds me of a politician. He always seems to promise more than he delivers.

★ ★ ★

The young woman was telling Santa what she wanted for Christmas.

"I'd like a new sports car," she said, "and a new wardrobe, and plenty of new jewelry, and a new mink coat."

"Alright," Santa replied, "but I'll have to check to make sure you were a real good girl all year."

"In that case," the young woman said, "how about if I settle for a Timex?"

Hotels and Motels

Angry Woman to Hotel Clerk: I thought this was supposed to be a respectable hotel!

Clerk: Yes, ma'am. Is something bothering you?

Woman: Yes! I just saw your handyman chasing a beautiful young girl past my room, trying to kiss her!

Clerk: Oh-oh! Did he catch her?

Woman: . . . No . . .

Clerk: Well, then, we're still a respectable hotel.

★ ★ ★

The woman couldn't help looking around at the shabby, unclean conditions as she approached the hotel desk.

"Is this the only hotel in this area?" she asked the desk clerk.

"Yeah," came the gruff answer.

"Well," the woman continued, "if this is the only hotel around, I guess I want to rent a room for the night."

"Do you have reservations?"

"I most certainly do! But I have to sleep somewhere, don't I?"

★ ★ ★

Angry Woman to Hotel Desk Clerk: What in the world was all that noise last night? I couldn't get to sleep 'til after midnight!

Desk Clerk: I'm sorry, ma'am, but we were holding an Elks' convention.

Woman: Well, next time, try holding it by the antlers!

★ ★ ★

Bellman to Hotel Manager: The family in room 312 wants you to send up a rabbit's foot.

Manager: A rabbit's foot? How come?

Bellman: They're superstitious about sleeping thirteen in a bed.

★ ★ ★

Incoming Customer to Hotel Desk Clerk: Eighty dollars?! Your sign outside says, "All Rooms, Fifty Dollars Per Day!"

Desk Clerk: Yes, but nights are thirty dollars extra.

★ ★ ★

"Desk clerk, there are two mice fighting in my room."

"What do you want for fifteen dollars—Mike Tyson?"

* * *

"Does this hotel have a golf course?"
"No."
"Then why does my sheet have eighteen holes in it?"

* * *

Man to Hotel Desk Clerk: Fifty dollars is too much for a room in a dumpy hotel like this.
Desk Clerk: Why, sir, the view alone is worth twenty dollars.
Man: How about I pay you thirty dollars and promise not to look?

* * *

Hotel Customer to Desk Clerk: One of the walls in my room is so thin, you can almost see through it.
Desk Clerk: That's your window.

* * *

Desk Clerk to Incoming Guest: Wait a minute, Mr. Smith. You signed the register with nothing but an "O."
Mr. Smith: Well, I usually sign with an "X," but I'm traveling under an alias.

* * *

"Desk clerk, that room you just rented me stinks."
"I'm sorry, sir. The last man who rented that room smuggled in his pet monkey. Why don't you try opening the window?"
"What? And lose all my pigeons?!"

* * *

"Where are you staying?"
"Oh, I got a room at the Z."
"The 'Z?' Where's that?"
"It's right behind the Y."

* * *

"Hello, room service? I want a breakfast of two eggs burned black around the edges, undercooked bacon, weak coffee, watery orange juice, and cold, hard, unbuttered toast."

"Why in the world do you want a terrible breakfast like that?"

"I'm homesick."

★ ★ ★

"I want a room for me and my billygoat."

"Billygoat? You can't bring a goat in here. What about the smell?"

"He'll get used to it."

★ ★ ★

"I want thirty gallons of milk sent up to my room."

"Thirty gallons of milk? What on earth for?"

"I want to take a milk bath."

"All right. Do you want it pasteurized?"

"No, no. Just up to my chin."

★ ★ ★

"I have another complaint about that room you rented me."

"Oh, for Pete's sake! What's eating you this time?"

"That's exactly what I'd like to know."

★ ★ ★

"Hello? Front desk? Tomorrow morning, I want breakfast in bed."

"All right, but you'll have to carry your bed down to the restaurant."

★ ★ ★

"Does this hotel have a swimming pool?"

"Yes, sir. Swimming is permitted all day, except between three and four o'clock in the afternoon."

"Why not then?"

"Because that's when we wash the sheets."

★ ★ ★

"Hold it, Mr. Smith. You haven't paid for your room yet."
"I didn't have a room. You ignored my reservation last night, and I had to sleep on the pool table."
"Well, that'll be two dollars an hour."

Hunting

"I used to hunt grizzly bears with a club."
"I don't believe that."
"Why not?"
"Because it's too dangerous, hunting grizzly bears with a club."
"Well, I don't do it anymore, anyway."
"Why not?"
"The membership fees got too high."

★ ★ ★

Two hunters were struggling to pull their bagged deer through the underbrush by its hind feet. A third hunter came along and noticed the antlers kept getting snarled in the weeds.

The third hunter suggested it would be easier to pull the deer by its antlers. The first two hunters decided to try it.

It worked. After pulling for a while, the first hunter said to the second, "That was a great idea. We're making good time now."

"Maybe so," said the second hunter, "but look how far we're getting from camp."

★ ★ ★

"Last time I went hunting, a bird flew right into my hiding place."
"Duck?"
"No, hit me right in the face."

★ ★ ★

"Do you mean to tell me that you jumped on the back of a wild grizzly bear and rode it like a bucking bronco?!"

"Yep. I tried to run, but it caught up to me, and just before it jumped on me, I spun around, grabbed onto its furry neck, and flipped myself up on its back."

"Whew! That sounds like a mighty scary thing to do!"

"Oh, that wasn't the scary part."

"It wasn't?"

"No. The scary part was getting off."

★ ★ ★

"How was your hunting trip?"

"That bird dog you loaned me ruined the whole trip."

"What? That's impossible. That dog loves to hunt."

"Oh, yeah? He knocked over my shotgun and blew a hole in the back of my new pickup truck."

"Well, I said he loved to hunt. I didn't say he was a good shot."

★ ★ ★

Any duck flying slow enough for him to shoot has to be too old to eat.

★ ★ ★

The two hunters had just settled into their duck blind as dawn began breaking.

"I wish I'd brung the television set with me," said the first hunter.

"The television set?" exclaimed the second. "Why the devil do you wish you'd brought the television set?"

"Because I left the ammo on it."

★ ★ ★

"How come I can't go turkey hunting with you?"

"Because the game warden told me my limit is one turkey at a time."

★ ★ ★

"How would you like to go hunting bear with me?"
"No, silly, the mosquitos would eat us up."

★ ★ ★

"I hear the rabbit hunting was good last season."
"It sure was. I ate so much rabbit meat, everytime I heard a dog bark I ran under a brushpile."

★ ★ ★

"Be careful with that shotgun! It might go off!"
"Don't worry. I'm covering the trigger with my finger."

★ ★ ★

Wife to Husband: How come you never take me duck hunting with you?
Husband: Because a good duck hunter has to know how to keep her trap shut.

★ ★ ★

"You say old Howler was the best hunting dog you ever saw?"
"No doubt about it. Once, me and Howler was quail huntin', and Howler burrowed into this big ol' brushpile, and out come a quail, and I got it. Pretty soon, out come another quail and, and I got it; then out come another quail and I got it, then out come another one, and I got it. . . ."
"Wait a minute. I've never known quail to take off one at a time. I thought they all took off at once."
"So did I, so after I'd got my limit I dug into that brushpile to see what was going on. Old Howler had trapped them quail in a rabbit hole and covered 'em with his paws. He was lettin' 'em out one at a time to make 'em easier to shoot."

★ ★ ★

First Duck Hunter: That mountain lion almost killed me! Why didn't you shoot?!
Second Duck Hunter: Because, silly, this is a bird gun.

Hypochondria/Hypochondriacs

"Do you remember Old Lady Johnson?"
"Do you mean the Miss Johnson who's always complaining about her health, always thinking she's sick?"
"That's her. Now she thinks she's dead."

★ ★ ★

She's the kind of person who lies awake for hours worrying about getting insomnia.

Ice Skating

"Where do you ice skate around here?"
"I don't ice skate."
"But if you did ice skate, where would you do it?"
"Probably on the same spot where I do my horseback riding."

★ ★ ★

"The last time she went ice skating, even the ice made funny cracks."

Indians

"I hear he's a full-blooded Sioux indian."
"Funny, he doesn't look Sioux-ish."

★ ★ ★

"My grandfather was a full-blooded Indian. He belonged to the Anonymous Indians."
"Never heard of them."

★ ★ ★

101 ———————————————————— INFIDELITY

"Look at that Indian smoke signal! What's it saying?"
"It says, 'Help! My souvenir shop's on fire!'"

Infidelity

"Say! How come my wife was sitting on your lap at that party last night?"
"I guess because I got there before the other fellows."

★ ★ ★

"Lemme get this straight, officer. You say you almost arrested a fellow for making love to his own wife?"
"Well, I didn't know it was his wife until they identified themselves. Besides, when I first got here, he tried to run for it."
"If it was his wife, why'd he run?"
"Because, until I turned on my flashlight, he didn't know it was her either."

★ ★ ★

First Man: Look! There's your wife, kissing a friend of yours!
Second Man: The joke's on you. I've never met that guy.

★ ★ ★

First Young Man: I've heard there are two women for every
    man in this country.
Second Young Man: If that's true, why did Charlie marry such
    a big fat girl?
First Young Man: I guess he wanted both of his women in one
    lump.

★ ★ ★

Young Man: Do you believe in love at first sight?
Young Woman: No, but on the other hand, I've never met
    Clint Black with his pockets full of thousand-dollar-bills.

★ ★ ★

The husband beckoned his wife over to his deathbed.

"Darling, I can't go to meet my maker with a guilty conscience," he whispered. "I must tell you I was unfaithful to you."

"Don't worry, dear," his wife answered. "I know all about that."

"You do?" he asked.

"Of course," the wife replied. "Why do you think I poisoned you?"

★ ★ ★

Wife to Husband: Did anyone ever tell you that you were the handsomest man in the county?

Husband: Why, no, they didn't.

Wife: Well, did anyone ever tell you that you were the best dancer in the county?

Husband: No, they never did.

Wife: Well, did anyone ever tell you that you were absolutely irresistible to women?

Husband: No . . .

Wife: Then what gave you all those crazy ideas last night at the party?

★ ★ ★

"You say your wife ran off with your best friend?"

"That's right."

"What's his name?"

"I don't know. I never met him."

★ ★ ★

"I got a note in the mail saying that if I didn't stop seeing this fellow's wife, he was going to shoot me."

"Then you'd better stop seeing her."

"I would, but he didn't sign his name."

★ ★ ★

"How long has Charlie been wearing a bra?"

"Since his wife found it in his glove compartment."

★ ★ ★

Wife to Husband: The man next door kisses his wife at least three times a day. Why can't you be so romantic?
Husband: All right, but let me get to know her better.

★ ★ ★

Husband to Wife: If I were to die, do you think you'd get married again?
Wife: Oh, probably.
Husband: Would you and your new husband live in this house?
Wife: I don't know, I never thought about it. I guess we would, yes.
Husband: Would you let him wear my clothes?
Wife: Well, I suppose so, yes.
Husband: And how about my golf clubs? Would you let him use my new golf clubs?
Wife: No. He's left-handed.

★ ★ ★

First Woman: How did you like your vacation?
Second Woman: It was all right, but tell me all about the scandals that went on while I was gone.
First Woman: Honey, while you were gone, there weren't any scandals.

★ ★ ★

"Does she still believe her husband goes to the dog races every Friday night?"
"Nope. Not since one of the dogs called him at home."

★ ★ ★

Angry First Man: Look at this picture and tell me what you see.
Second Man: That's me and your wife dancing.
First Man: Uh-huh, and look at this other picture and tell what you see.
Second Man: That's me and your wife kissing on the beach.

First Man: Well? What are you going to do about these pictures?

Second Man: I'll take three of those, billfold size, and one of those, eight-by-ten.

Inflation

If groceries get any more expensive, we'll be carrying the money in the shopping cart and the groceries in our purse.

Inheritances

Wife to Husband: If you inherited a lot of money, would you split with me?

Husband: If I inherited a lot of money, I'd split with you in a minute.

In-Laws

My wife knows there are two sides to every story—hers and her mother's.

★ ★ ★

"On your picnic, I thought it was very considerate of your husband to warn your mother to stay back from that cliff."

"Mother was carrying the lunch basket."

★ ★ ★

Man to Daughter's Suitor: The man who marries my daughter will need a lot of money.

Daughter's Suitor: Then I'm perfect for her.

★ ★ ★

"I just hate it that my mother-in-law lives with my wife and me."

"Why don't you ask her to move?"

"I would, but it's her house."

★ ★ ★

Husband to Wife: Your mama's starting to look like my pit bull, Fang.

Wife: Shhh! Don't you care about hurting somebody's feelings?

Husband: Don't worry about that. Fang's down at the barn.

★ ★ ★

"I understand you want to become my son-in-law."

"No, sir, I certainly don't. But I want to marry your daughter, and I can't think of any way out of it."

★ ★ ★

The only good thing my mother-in-law ever did was object to my marriage.

★ ★ ★

Wife to Husband: Let me remind you that my grandfather fought with General Douglas MacArthur!

Husband: Aw, your family will fight with anybody.

★ ★ ★

"You say you were run over by a car from behind in the middle of the night, in a driving rainstorm, and yet you're sure it was your mother-in-law driving the car?"

"That's right."

"Remember, sir, you are under oath! How can you be so certain?"

"I recognized the laugh."

★ ★ ★

You say he's planning to marry his ex-wife's sister?
Yeah, that way he won't have to break in a new mother-in-law.

★ ★ ★

Wife to Husband: Do you think I favor my mother?
Husband: Yeah, but that's not what I call a favor.

Insomnia

The best cure for insomnia is to get plenty of sleep.

Insurance

"Do you have insurance?"
"Yes."
"Accident?"
"No, I bought it on purpose."

★ ★ ★

"He and his wife are going to collect plenty on that car accident in front of their house."
"Wait a minute. They weren't in that accident."
"No, but his wife thought fast enough to break three of his ribs."

Inventions

"I hear your cousin invented a new acid that will eat through absolutely anything."

"Yep. Now he's trying to invent something to keep it in."

★ ★ ★

"The Thermos bottle is the greatest invention in history."

"Why in the world would you say that?"

"Because if you put something cold in it, it keeps it cold. And if you put something hot in it, it keeps it hot."

"What's so great about that?"

"Well, how does it know?"

Iran

After a meeting with his twelve cabinet ministers, Iran's Ayatollah discovered his briefcase was missing. He called his secret police and asked them to pick up the twelve men for questioning.

The next morning, he found his briefcase beside his bed and realized he hadn't taken it to the meeting at all.

He called the chief of his secret police, told him it was a mistake, and ordered him to release any of the ministers he might be holding.

"You're too late, Your Holiness," the chief told him. "They've all confessed."

Jealousy

Wife to Husband: I'll have you know, when I was a young girl, I used to make all my boyfriends jealous.

Husband: Yeah, they got jealous when they saw somebody else's girlfriend.

"... And-then-there's-the-one-about-the-traveling-sales-man-who-stops-at-the-farmhouse-and-knocks-on-the-door-and ..."

Jokes

"Did you write some of the jokes in this book?"
"Yes, I did."
"Gee, you must be older than you look."

★ ★ ★

There's a good lesson to be learned from this book: Not all bum jokes are about hoboes.

★ ★ ★

The trouble with telling somebody a good joke is that it reminds them of a bad joke.

★ ★ ★

"Speaking of funny stories, do you have time for a couple of real doozies?"
"Sure."
"Doozie! Doozie!"

Juries

Jury: Twelve people brought together to decide which side has the best lawyer.

Karate

"I hear your cousin, the expert in karate, got beat up."
"Yeah, the other guy was an expert in kaballbat."

Kissing

She kisses like she's taking a bite out of a leaky fried egg sandwich.

★ ★ ★

He's hard to understand. He didn't kiss his wife for over a year, then he got mad when I did.

★ ★ ★

"She claims to be saving her kisses."
"Humph! Then, by now, she's got the biggest collection in town."

★ ★ ★

"There were over two hundred boys in my graduating class, and I never kissed one of them."
"Which one was that?"

★ ★ ★

She's saving her kisses for the men she marries.

★ ★ ★

"Am I the first man you ever kissed?"
"Could be . . . were you at the 1983 Mardi Gras?"

★ ★ ★

"I have this uncontrollable desire to kiss men with beards."
"Would you like to meet my psychiatrist?"
"Does he have a beard?"

★ ★ ★

"Are you going to let Fred kiss you tonight?"
"I don't know. There are so many germs in the average kiss."
"Don't worry. Fred's kisses are way below average."

★ ★ ★

"I let Freddy kiss me last night."
"Was it a moment of weakness?"
"No, it was more like an hour and a half of weakness."

★ ★ ★

On their first date, the young man asked the girl for a kiss.
"I wouldn't dream of letting a man kiss me unless I was engaged," she answered. "But don't worry about that, I've been engaged lots of times."

★ ★ ★

Catholic Nun to Catholic High School Girl: Sally, I want you to know, it didn't look good, letting that strange man kiss you in public.
Student: Well, Sister, it was better than it looked.

★ ★ ★

Woman to Hired Gardener: Sir, ever since I hired you to work on my garden, I've been afraid you're going to try to force me to kiss you.
Gardener: Lady, how could I force you to kiss me with this shovel in one hand and this bag of peat moss in the other hand?
Woman: Well, you could set the peat moss over there and lean the shovel against that tree.

★ ★ ★

"My last girlfriend would think nothing of kissing me ten times a day."
"I don't blame her. I wouldn't think much of it, either."

★ ★ ★

"Susie, did you say Fred doesn't know how to kiss?"
"Not exactly. I said he *didn't* know how to kiss."

★ ★ ★

"If I try to kiss you, will you call for help?"
"I don't know. Will you need help?"

★ ★ ★

"I caught my husband kissing!"
"That's exactly how I caught mine."

Landlords

"I sold my house last week."
"Are you happy with the price you got for it?"
"Yeah, but, boy, is my landlord upset."

★ ★ ★

"On my vacation, I toured Abraham Lincoln's boyhood home. It's exactly as it was over a hundred years ago."
"We must have the same landlord."

Language/Languages

"When you were in Europe, did you have any trouble with your French?"
"No, but those French people sure did."

★ ★ ★

He claims to be multilingual—he can speak Southern.

★ ★ ★

"I have degrees in English, French, Spanish, and algebra."
"Say something funny in algebra."

Laundry

I still send my shirts to an old fashion laundry. They tear off the buttons by hand.

Lawsuits

"The McFlynn's are suing the builder who built their house. He forgot to put in a bathtub."

"Wait a minute. They moved into that house over a year ago."

"Yeah, but they didn't miss it 'til last month."

★ ★ ★

Judge to Litigant: You say this fellow drove through your fence, knocked down your mailbox, smashed your plastic lawn flamingos, bounced off your porch, and ran into the pickup truck in your yard?

Litigant: That's right, your honor.

Judge: Are you suing for damages?

Litigant: Shoot, no! I got enough damages! I'm suing for repairs.

Lawyers

Every morning, the fellow saw his lawyer neighbor riding a bicycle to the commuter station while the lawyer's wife ran along behind, sweating, panting, struggling to keep up.

Finally, the fellow asked the lawyer why he rode the bicycle while his wife had to run.

"Simple," the lawyer answered, "She doesn't have a bicycle."

★ ★ ★

"What's the difference between a lawyer and a vulture?"
"Jewelry."

★ ★ ★

"I've decided to make an honest living by becoming a lawyer."
"Well, you won't have much competition."

★ ★ ★

Why is it, a lawyer writes a five-thousand-word document, then calls it a "brief"?

★ ★ ★

I borrowed twenty thousand dollars from my dad to pay my way through law school. My first case was when my dad sued for me for twenty thousand dollars.

★ ★ ★

Talk's cheap, unless it's a lawyer talking.

Laziness

"Have you been sleeping good lately?"
"Oh, I slept all right last night and pretty good this morning. But I tossed and turned all afternoon."

★ ★ ★

He was so lazy, he was dead for two weeks before anybody noticed.

★ ★ ★

He's very superstitious about manual labor. He won't work any week with a Friday in it.

★ ★ ★

That man is too lazy to sweat.

★ ★ ★

What time he can spare from figuring out how to get out of work on the job, he devotes to thinking up ways to avoid chores around the house.

★ ★ ★

The only thing I've ever seen him do quickly is get tired.

★ ★ ★

"Look out that window and see if it's still raining outside."
"Too much trouble. Just call in the dog and see if he's wet."

★ ★ ★

She was so lazy as a child, she played step rope.

★ ★ ★

The trouble with laying around doing nothing is you're never quite sure when you're finished.

★ ★ ★

I'm at that awkward age: Too old to live off my parents and too young to collect Social Security.

★ ★ ★

"You look mighty tired today, Grandpa."
"Yeah, I dreamed I had a job."

★ ★ ★

"I hear your lazy cousin claims he's an artist."
"Yeah. He picked it because nobody can prove he ain't."

Loans

"Listen, I need fifty dollars."

"Fifty dollars?"

"Yeah, and I have no idea where I can get it."

"That's a relief! I was afraid you might have an idea you could borrow it from me."

★ ★ ★

"Hello, is this Fred?"

"Yes, this is Fred."

"Are you sure? It doesn't sound like Fred."

"Yes, I'm absolutely sure. This is Fred."

"Fred, this is Charlie. Will you loan me fifty dollars 'til the end of the month?"

"I'll tell Fred you called just as soon as he comes in."

★ ★ ★

"Thinking of Fred Johnson always reminds me of Charlie Renfro."

"Why's that?"

"Because they both owe me ten dollars."

★ ★ ★

"Are you going to be using your lawn mower Saturday?"

"Yes."

"Good. I need to borrow your car."

Logic

"If it takes two gardeners two hours to dig two holes, how long does it take one gardener to dig half a hole?"

"You can't dig half a hole."

★ ★ ★

"Why can't a man who lives in the United States be buried in Canada?"
"Because he's not dead."

Lonely Hearts' Clubs

She sent her picture to a lonely hearts' club, but they weren't that lonely.

Lying

"You know, George Washington could not tell a lie."
"Yes, but I have a much higher standard than that."
"You do?"
"Yes. I could tell them, all right—but I don't."
—Mark Twain

Magazines

There's a new girlie magazine for married men only. The centerfold is the same girl, month after month after month after month. . . .

★ ★ ★

"What would you do if you bought a girlie magazine and found your wife's picture in it?"
"Get my money back."

★ ★ ★

He: Would you ever appear in *Playboy* magazine?
She: Yes and no.
He: What does that mean?
She: Well, part of me would and part of me wouldn't.

Malapropisms

(Malapropisms are twists of the language that, somehow, make sense even though they are seemingly senseless. Does that make sense?)

Include me out.

Nowadays, every Tom, Dick, and Harry is named Mike.

In two words, im possible.

If people don't want to come to your party, nobody can stop them.

This feels like déjà vu all over again.

That restaurant is so crowded, nobody goes there anymore.

Either way, you win or lose.

It ain't that I'm pessimistic; it's just that we ain't got a chance.

For your information, I would like to ask a question.

The future just ain't what it used to be.

I feel a draft. Raise that window down.

All right, I want you to listen very slowly. . . .

A verbal contract isn't worth the paper it's written on.

Marriage

"What's the secret to your long, happy marriage?"
"My wife and I go out for a romantic dinner at least once a week."
"That's wonderful! Where do you go?"
"I like Italian . . . I don't know where she goes."

★ ★ ★

"How did you meet your husband?"
"I was crossing a street when this car drove up and stopped with a big jerk. It was him."

★ ★ ★

"I hear she met her husband in a department store."
"Yeah, at the remnant counter."

★ ★ ★

I'm not sure if I'm staying married for love or for spite.

★ ★ ★

"Sir, your daughter is going to marry me."
"It's your own fault for hanging around here so much."

★ ★ ★

"I knew he was in big trouble when I went to his wedding."
"How's that?"
"Well, the minister asked the bride if she took this man to be her husband, and she said, 'I do.' Then the minister asked the groom if he took this woman to be his wife, and she said, 'He does.'"

★ ★ ★

Wife to Husband: Before we were married, you said nothing was good enough for me.
Husband: Yeah, and I was right.

★ ★ ★

The only reason some people get married is to have somebody to blame.

★ ★ ★

"I just had a fellow do me out of half a million dollars."
"What happened?"
"He wouldn't let me marry his daughter."

★ ★ ★

A wife is someone who'll stick by you through all the problems you wouldn't have had if you hadn't married her in the first place.

★ ★ ★

I took her for better or worse, but she's worse than I took her for.

★ ★ ★

Husband to Wife: I invited a friend home for supper.
Wife: What? Are you crazy? The house is a mess, I didn't go shopping, all the dishes are dirty, and I don't feel like cooking!
Husband: I know all that.
Wife: Then why'd you invite a friend for supper?
Husband: Because the poor fool's thinking about getting married.

★ ★ ★

"He asked Linda to marry him."
"Did she say 'yes' or 'no'?"
"Neither. She said '*Yuck!*'"

★ ★ ★

"Did you know that almost half of all marriages end in divorce?"
"What do the other half end in?"

★ ★ ★

It's not hard at all to catch a husband. The trick is, to catch a single fellow.

★ ★ ★

Husband to Wife: Do you ever look at a man and wish you were single again?
Wife: Yes, every morning.

★ ★ ★

"My Aunt Tillie could have married anybody she pleased."
"Then why didn't she ever get married?"
"Because she never pleased anybody."

When to Propose . . . or Not

Men who can answer "yes" to five or more of these questions should consider carefully before proposing marriage.

- In the kitchen, has she ever referred to an oven as "that square thing"?

- Does she use the phrase "you know" more than twice per sentence?

- Is she making monthly payments of more than $300 to a plastic surgeon?

- Have you noticed her name tattooed on three or more local bikers?

- Have you noticed three or more local bikers' names tatooed on her?

- Does she regularly compare your love-making talents to an old boyfriend's?

- Does she regularly compare your love-making talents to the Green Bay Packers?

- If she works as a check-out clerk at K-Mart, a band teller, or a cashier in an all-night diner, did she bet more than $10,000 on the last Super Bowl?

- Does she have a wholesale source for Deodorant-in-a-Drum?

- Has she ever used the word *poo-poo*?

- If forced to use it at all, does she choose to spell the word *sex*?

- Does her job resumé include a six-year stint at Big Leg Emma's House Of Painful Delights?

"... And then the television broke last week, and I warned you about that brand, and those nasty oily tools of yours are still lying all over the garage, and I have to paint the screens again because you wouldn't buy aluminum screens like I told you to, and I can't find the paint brushes because you didn't put them away in the correct place, and ..."

When to Accept A Proposal . . . or Not

Women who can answer "yes" to five or more of these questions should consider carefully before accepting a proposal of marriage.

• On his first date with you, did he pick you up early so you could help with his laundry?

• To reach him in an emergency, would anyone think to call the local adult bookstore?

• Has he ever bragged about seeing every episode of "Gilligan's Island" at least four times?

• Is it unclear to some people whether that's a mustache or just a lot of unruly nose hair?

• Is his idea of a classy restaurant one where every table has its own stack of ketchup packets?

• Does his car get more than sixty miles per gallon?

• Does the label on his deodorant include the phrase "Industrial Strength?

• Has he memorized the telephone number of at least one bail-bondsman?

★ ★ ★

Wife to Husband: What do you say we go out tonight and have a good time?
Husband: Good idea. And if you get home first, turn on the porch light.

★ ★ ★

"She's marrying a doctor she met when she went in for X-rays."
"I wonder what he saw in her?"

★ ★ ★

Husband to Wife: If I die, I want you to marry Grady Renfro.
Wife: How come?
Husband: Because years ago, he sold me a lame horse.

★ ★ ★

Wife to Husband: If you had it all to do over again, would you still get married?
Husband: Yeah, I suppose I would; if I could find the right woman.

★ ★ ★

Wife to Husband: I feel like taking a long, quiet walk in the moonlight.
Husband: Good idea. Take the dog with you.

Mechanics

Man to Mechanic: Excuse me, sir. Are you familiar with driving a Mercedes?
Mechanic: If I was familiar with driving a Mercedes, would I be working here?

★ ★ ★

Man: How much would you charge to fix my car?
Mechanic: What's wrong with it?
Man: I'm not sure.
Mechanic: Twelve hundred dollars.

Memorials

"George Washington was most famous for his memory."
"What in the world makes you think that?"
"Because our government built a monument to it."

Memory

There's one good thing about being absentminded: You can hide your own Easter eggs.

★ ★ ★

"I have a terrible time remembering names and faces, but that's not all bad."
"It's not?"
"No, just think how many new people I get to meet."

Microwave Ovens

Every morning, I wake up late but then I make instant coffee in my microwave oven. It throws me back in time seven minutes.

Miscellaneous

"What would you like to do today?"
"I'm not sure. Let's think . . ."
"No, let's do something you can do, too."

★ ★ ★

That woman is so bow-legged, you could hang her over the barn door for luck.

★ ★ ★

"I keep thinking today is Saturday."
"Today *is* Saturday."
"No wonder I keep thinking that."

★ ★ ★

That woman is so two-faced, she could sing a duet.

Money

"I wish I had enough money to buy a hundred goats."
"Why in the world do you want a hundred goats?"
"I don't want a hundred goats."
"But you just said you wish you had enough money to buy a hundred goats!"
"Right . . . if I had that much money, I could buy a pickup truck."

★ ★ ★

Every week, she rents a goat for two dollars, then tells her husband she paid fifteen dollars to have the grass mowed.

★ ★ ★

A fellow holding five twenty-dollar bills stopped a wealthy-looking lady as she was leaving the store.
"Excuse me, lady," he said, "but did you lose a hundred-dollar bill back there?"
The lady quickly checked her purse and replied, "Why, yes, I did. But those are twenties."
"Well," the man explained, "I figured you might want to give me a reward."

★ ★ ★

I have enough money to last the rest of my life, so long as I die by Thursday.

★ ★ ★

"Last Sunday, I found a wallet packed with money down by the church."
"Did you give it back?"
"Not yet. I'm still trying to decide if it's a temptation from the devil or the answer to a prayer."

★ ★ ★

Whoever said that money couldn't buy happiness just didn't know where to shop.

★ ★ ★

"Did you ever wish for enough money to pay for everything you wanted?"
"Shoot, I just wish for enough money to pay for everything I've already bought."

★ ★ ★

I'm so broke, if a robber was to rob me, all he'd get would be practice.

★ ★ ★

The great thing about money is, no matter what you're wearing, it doesn't clash.

★ ★ ★

My laundry wants me to pay my bill, and my broker wants more money on margin. Either way, I lose my shirt.

Monogamy

Monogamy: Having only one wife—and hardly any girl-friends at all.

Moonshine/Moonshiners

"I hear whiskey broke up their happy home."
"Sort of. The still in their kitchen exploded."

Motorcycles/Motorcyclists

"Why do motorcycle gangs wear black leather?"
"Because white chiffon is too easy to wrinkle."

Movies

"I wish I understood those ratings they put on movies."
"No problem. 'G' means nobody gets the girl; 'PG' means the hero gets the girl; 'R' means the bad guy gets the girl; and 'NC-17' means everybody gets the girl."

Music/Musicians

"I've played music in most every nightspot in Nashville."
"Why did you stop?"
"I ran out of quarters."

★ ★ ★

"How did your concert go last night?"
"Well, I decided to have a theme."
"A theme?"
"Uh-huh. I decided to make every song relate in some way to fruit. I opened with 'In The Shade of the Old Apple Tree,' then I played 'Yes, We Have No Bananas,' then I did 'When It's Peach Pickin' Time Down in Georgia.'"
"Did the audience like that idea?"
"I'm not sure—they threw tomatoes."

★ ★ ★

"I just cleaned out my attic, and threw away an old guitar with the word 'Elvis' scratched on the back."

"Good heavens, man! That sounds like Elvis Presley's very first guitar! That thing was worth a fortune!"

"Naw, it couldn't have been worth much. Some guy named Hank Williams ruined it by scratching 'Good Luck' on the side."

★ ★ ★

"Did you start out in life as a guitar player?"

"No, I started out as a baby."

★ ★ ★

"Why did you switch from playing the violin to the piano?"

"Because a glass of beer won't slide off a piano."

★ ★ ★

"All the members of my band were hand-picked."

"Next time, wait 'till they're ripe."

★ ★ ★

Does your band take requests?"

"Sure, what would you like us to play?"

"Checkers."

★ ★ ★

"You can get a lot of beautiful music out of a violin like this."

"Yeah, but somebody got it all out before they gave it to you."

★ ★ ★

"I just recorded a new album, and they tell me that album is going to be responsible for the sale of thousands of CD players."

"I'm not surprised. I know I'm gonna sell mine."

★ ★ ★

"What did you want to be when you were a little boy?"

"Well, I decided I was too short to be a basketball player and too heavy to be a jockey and too slow to be a runner. I figured I was built just right to be a guitar player."

★ ★ ★

"I'm going to New York to continue my trumpet lessons."

"Sounds pretty expensive. Where did you get the money?"

"My neighbors chipped in."

★ ★ ★

"Why was the crowd so small at my concert last night? Wasn't it advertised that I was going to perform?"

"No, but word must have leaked out."

★ ★ ★

"Grandpa's been playing the fiddle since he was a little boy. That's a long time."

"Yep. When he first started, it was called 'New Wave' music."

★ ★ ★

"I see you've borrowed the neighbor lady's trumpet. I didn't know you could play the trumpet?"

"I can't. But while I've got it, neither can she."

Names

"My folks named my brother after my rich uncle Bill."

"I didn't know you had a brother named Bill."

"I don't. His name is Stingy Old Tightwad."

★ ★ ★

"It's a good thing your parents named you 'Charlie.'"

"Why's that?"

"Because that's what everybody calls you."

★ ★ ★

"What was your mother's name before she was married?"
"I didn't have a mother before she was married."

Narcolepsy

My doctor called to tell me my tests came back. He says I
don't have narcolepsy. I'm just sleepy.

Newspapers

Woman to Newspaper Obituary Editor: I want to run an an-
nouncement in your obituaries: My husband died of a shotgun wound.
Editor: That's terrible! When did it happen?
Woman: Just as soon as I find him!

★ ★ ★

He's so old-fashioned his favorite newspaper is USA Yesterday.

★ ★ ★

"Did you see the front-page story about me in the morning
paper?"
"You? You made the front page?"
"Yep, I sure did."
"What's it about?"
"Well, the headline reads, 'Unemployed People on Rise.'"

Nudity/Nudists

She had more goosebumps on her than two nudists in a snow storm.

★ ★ ★

One Nudist to Another: Will we be dressing for dinner?

★ ★ ★

Where do nudists carry their car keys?

★ ★ ★

Wife to Husband: If you don't get me some new clothes, I'm gonna start running around buck naked! What will the neighbors think about that?!
Husband: They'll probably think I married you for your money.

★ ★ ★

"Why did you break up with that nudist fellow you were dating?"
"Because he wanted us to start seeing too much of each other."

Optimism/Optimists

Optimist: That's a ninety-year-old bridegroom shopping for a house close to a school.

★ ★ ★

An optimist is a person who doesn't understand the enormity of the problem.

★ ★ ★

An optimist is a fellow who goes shopping for a suit to be buried in and gets one with two pairs of pants.

Parachuting

"Is it true you took your blind Uncle Charlie skydiving, and he loved it?"

"Yep. He said it was the funnest thing he'd ever done."

"Do you plan to take him again?"

"No chance."

"But if he enjoyed it, why not?"

"Have you ever heard a German shepherd scream at 20,000 feet?"

★ ★ ★

"How does a blind skydiver know when he's going to land?"

"The leash goes slack."

★ ★ ★

"I just graduated from skydiving school."

"How many successful jumps did you have to make?"

"All of them."

Peeping Toms

"My wife caught a Peeping Tom last night, and she'd have killed him if we hadn't stopped her."

"He must have made her very angry, peeking at her, huh?"

"No, that's not what made her the maddest."

"It's not?"

"No, she got mad when he reached in the window and closed the curtains."

Perfume

The clerk showed the fellow the store's most expensive perfume.

"This is called 'Perhaps'," the sales clerk said. "It's $285 per ounce."

"Listen," the fellow shot back. "For $285 per ounce, I don't want something called 'Perhaps'; I want something called 'You Can Bet Your Sweet Bippy On It'."

Pessimism/Pessimists

A pessimist is an optimist who's been to Las Vegas.

★ ★ ★

"You say you've sworn to never go anywhere again with your cousin, the incurable pessimist?"

"Yep. He and I went to the circus the other day, and he ruined the whole trip."

"How so?"

"Well, we watched a fellow come walking out on a wire fifty feet in the air, stand on one foot, blindfolded, twirl a hula hoop on one leg, and play 'Wildwood Flower' on a guitar behind his back while he sang."

"Wow! That sounds great!"

"That's exactly what I thought. I said, 'Now, Charlie, you have to admit, that fellow is a wonderful performer.'"

"What did Charlie say to that?"

"He said, 'I guess he ain't bad, but he's no Roy Clark.'"

Philosophy

He got an A in his philosophy class—he proved his teacher didn't exist.

Plastic Surgery

She's had so many face lifts, she's talking through her belly button.

★ ★ ★

She's had so many face lifts, when she smells something her forehead twitches.

★ ★ ★

She was going to have her face lifted, but when she found out what it costs, she dropped it.

Police

First Young Woman: You say you had a date with a policeman, and you allowed him to go too far?
Second Young Woman: I had no choice. He told me it's against the law to resist an officer.

★ ★ ★

He's the only person on the FBI's Least-Wanted List.

★ ★ ★

"If your grandfather was such a big-time bank robber, was he ever on the FBI's Ten Most-Wanted List?"
"No, but he got Honorable Mention."

Politics

"I used to eat a lot better back when Ronald Reagan was president."
"Oh. . . . So you think times were better back then?"
"No. . . . I had my own teeth."

★ ★ ★

Man to Senator: I wouldn't vote for you if you were living with Saint Peter himself.
Senator: If I were living with Saint Peter, you wouldn't be in my district.

★ ★ ★

Congressman to Young Lady: Which party are you affiliated with?
Young Lady: I can't tell you. The party I'm affiliated with isn't divorced yet.

★ ★ ★

"Why don't we ever hear of a thief burglarizing a politician's house?"
"Professional courtesy."

★ ★ ★

"I admit I was speeding, Your Honor, but I was on very important business. You see, I'm a United States Senator."
"Thirty days! Ignorance is no excuse!"

★ ★ ★

Last year the county spent $80,000 on a new school bus so kids wouldn't have to walk to school, and this year they're spending $200,000 on a new gymnasium so they can get some exercise.

★ ★ ★

"How can you tell if a senator is lying?"
"You can see his lips move."

★ ★ ★

The trouble with politicians is 90 percent of them are giving the other 10 percent a bad name.

★ ★ ★

"Four years ago, my cousin ran for state senator."
"What's he do now?"
"Nothing. He got elected."

★ ★ ★

"I know everything it takes to be a good politician."
"Liar."
"That's one of 'em."

★ ★ ★

"Last time I went to vote, a fella pulled a gun on me and asked if I was going to vote Republican or Democrat."
"What did you tell him?"
"After I thought about it, I told him to go ahead and shoot."

★ ★ ★

"If you were elected president, what would you do about defense?"
"I'd paint it the same color as de house."

★ ★ ★

Politics wouldn't be so bad if we could just get rid of the politicians.

★ ★ ★

"The politicians in Washington want us to believe that nuclear waste is perfectly safe, so long as we're careful where we put it."
"No problem. Let's put it under the White House."

★ ★ ★

"How's your political science homework going?"
"I need an example of an 'indirect tax'."
"How about a dog tax?"
"A dog tax? How is that an indirect tax?"
"Well, the dog doesn't pay it."

★ ★ ★

"Old man Johnson is losin' ground fast."
"Oh-oh. Health problems?"
"Nope. Tax problems."

★ ★ ★

Only a small percentage of criminals are sent to prison. A bigger percentage is re-elected.

Polls

In a recent poll, 78 percent of those polled said they disliked being polled.

Pool

"Even though the eight ball was tucked behind four other balls, I figured I could make the shot if I bounced the cue ball over the six ball on top of the ten ball, caromed it off the four ball and the side cushion, with enough spin to curve around the two-ball just tight enough to miss the ten ball after the ten ball came to rest."
"Did you make the shot?"
"No. I mis-cued."

Post Office

If the world keeps getting smaller everyday, why does the cost of a postage stamp keep going up?

Poverty

Our family was so poor . . .

. . . on Halloween, we went trick-or-treating every other year because my brother and I had to take turns using the costume.

. . . the only time we had plenty of meat was when the dog died.

. . . us five kids had to sleep in the same bed until my sister finally got married . . . that made six.

. . . I used to go home late so I could sleep on top.

Procrastination

Woman to Taxi Driver: You can procrastinate me at the next corner.
Taxi Driver: "Procrastinate" you? I don't know what you're talking about, lady.
Woman: "Procrastinate," dummy. It means "to put off."

★ ★ ★

"I'm so bad at putting things off, I finally joined 'Procrastinators Anonymous.'"
"Did that help?"
"Not yet, we haven't gotten around to having a meeting."

★ ★ ★

Starting next month, I'm going to stop putting things off.

Profit

People say, "A penny for your thoughts," but, on the other hand, they say they want to give you their "two cents' worth." Seems to me, somebody's making a profit on the deal.

Pronunciation

"How did things go at school today?"
"Not bad. Today we studied pronunkiation."

Psychiatry/Psychiatrists/Psychology/ Psychologists

"It's amazing how a psychiatrist like you can listen to those terrible tragedies your patients talk about all day, yet you stay in such a happy mood."
"It's not so amazing; I don't listen."

★ ★ ★

"Why do you seem so upset?"
"My wife introduced me to her psychiatrist this morning."
"So what?"
"So she said to him, 'Doctor, this is my husband. You know, one of the men I've been telling you about.'"

★ ★ ★

Patient to Psychiatrist: Have you figured out what's wrong with me yet, Doc?
Psychiatrist: Yes, Mr. Jones, you have a split personality.
Patient: Baloney, Doc. I don't believe that, and neither do I.

★ ★ ★

Patient to Psychiatrist: Listen, Doc, you've been trying unsuccessfully to cure my kleptomania for over a year. Isn't there something more I can do?
Psychiatrist: Yes. How about picking me up a car stereo?

★ ★ ★

"Has your cousin ever gotten over his kleptomania?"
"No, but he's still taking something for it."

★ ★ ★

A psychologist received this postcard from a vacationing patient: "Having a wonderful time. Why?"

★ ★ ★

A fellow went to a psychiatrist and told him he felt people were trying to take advantage of him.
"Don't worry about that," the psychiatrist told him. "Everybody feels like people are trying to take advantage of them now and then. You're completely normal."
"Gee, thanks, Doc," the fellow said. "I feel better already."
"Good," the psychiatrist answered. "That'll be two hundred dollars, and I need to borrow your car tonight."

★ ★ ★

"Doc, even though you've diagnosed me as having a split personality, is it all right for me to get married?"
"Oh, sure. Who are you planning to marry?"
"The Johnson twins."

★ ★ ★

"Doc, I always have the feeling that people don't like me and that they're out to get me. Does that mean I have an inferiority complex or a rejection complex?"
"Neither. It means your personality stinks."

★ ★ ★

"She finally went to a psychiatrist about her suicidal tendencies."
"Did he tell her he was confident about being able to cure her?"
"Well, first he made her pay in advance."

★ ★ ★

"Doc, my brother thinks he's a chicken."

"Don't worry, I can cure him. Bring him right in."

"Could we hold off for a week or so? Right now, we need the eggs."

★ ★ ★

Psychiatrist to Patient: I believe your depression is rooted in deep-seated feelings of hostility and inferiority, first manifested in childhood due to an overbearing mother and a rather docile father, but reinforced significantly by inhibiting extroverted siblings and a rather crowded home life.

Patient: But, doc . . . I'm not depressed.

Psychiatrist: I took a shot.

★ ★ ★

Patient to Psychiatrist: Doc, I had a terrible dream last night . . . I dreamed I died and went to see St. Peter, and he told me if I'd never cheated on my wife I could drive a luxury car around heaven forever. But he said if I'd cheated on her one time, I had to drive a mid-size car forever, and if I'd cheated twice I had to drive a compact car, and if I'd cheated three times I had to drive a sub-compact, and if I'd cheated . . .

Psychiatrist: Hold it! You've never cheated on your wife at all, have you?

Patient: Nope, and that's what I told Saint Peter, Doc. So he gave me this big luxury car with all the extras, and off I drove.

Psychiatrist: What's so bad about that? Sounds like a great dream to me.

Patient: Well, I was driving along in that thing and came on my wife. She was riding a bicycle with two flat tires.

★ ★ ★

Patient to Psychiatrist: Doc, every night I dream about teepees and wigwams. Teepees over here, wigwams over there. What's it mean?

Psychiatrist: It means you're too tense.

★ ★ ★

Male Patient to Psychiatrist: Doc, I had the worst dream of my life last night. I dreamed I was with twelve of the most beautiful chorus girls in the world. Blondes, brunettes, redheads, all dancing in a row . . .
Psychiatrist: Hold it, Fred. That doesn't sound so terrible.
Patient: Oh, yeah? In the dream, I was the third girl from the end.

★ ★ ★

Patient: Doc, I know it's crazy and silly, but I keep feeling that people tend to ignore me.
Psychiatrist: Next!

★ ★ ★

First Young Woman: Why did you break up with that psychiatrist you were seeing?
Second Young Woman: Because everytime I showed up late for a date he accused me of having hidden hostilities, and when I showed up early he accused me of having an anxiety complex, and when I was right on time he said I was exhibiting compulsive behavior.

Real Estate

"I got good news and bad news about that house I'm trying to buy."
"What's the good news?"
"The people accepted my offer of five hundred thousand dollars."
"What's the bad news?"
"They want fifty dollars down."

Recycling

"By the time old Cousin Mayburn died, he had an artificial leg, a transplanted heart, a plastic hip joint, a glass eye, a wig, a hearing aid, and store-bought teeth."
"Where did they bury him?"
"They didn't bury him. They recycled him."

Redundancies

Sign on government office:

Department of Redundancies Department

Reincarnation

A woman was worried whether or not her dead husband made it to heaven, so she decided to try to contact his spirit by having a seance.

Sure enough, after the usual mumbo-jumbo of calling to the spirits, her husband's voice was heard answering, "Hello, Margaret, this is meee . . ."

"Fred," she answered. "I just have to know if you're happy there in the afterlife. What's it like there?"

"Oooooh, it's much more beautiful here than I ever imagined," Fred answered. "The sky is bluer, the air is cleaner, and the pastures are much more lush and green than I ever expected. And the only things we do, all day long, are make love and eat, make love and eat, over and over."

"Thank God, you made it to heaven," his wife cried.

"Heaven?" he answered, "What heaven? I'm a buffalo in Montana."

Religion

At the old time tent revival, it was time for the preacher to heal the faithful. The first fellow hoping to be healed came to the minister on crutches.

"What's your name?" the minister asked.

"My name's Fred," the crippled man answered, "and I was born with deformed ankles. I've had to use crutches all my life."

"Fred," the minister boomed, "I want you to go behind that curtain and wait for my orders! The fine people in this audience will pray for your cure!"

Fred went behind the curtain as the next 'patient' approached the minister.

"What's your name?" the minister demanded.

"Mah name's Hauhwee," the fellow replied, "and Ah cain't tawk pwain. Ah bin to doctahs aw ovah da countwee, but dey cain't hep me."

"Harry," the minister ordered, "you go behind that curtain with Fred, and we'll pray for you, and you'll be cured!"

So Harry went behind the curtain with Fred, and the minister ordered the audience to begin praying with him for the two men's healing. Louder and louder the evangelist got, dancing around the pulpit in a frenzy of pleading prayer.

Finally, the minister stopped suddenly and called out, "Fred!"

The audience instantly fell silent, knowing the moment of truth had come.

"Fred," the evangelist repeated, "slide your left crutch out from under the curtain!"

After a couple beats of apprehensive silence, sure enough, the crutch came poking out from under the curtain.

"All right," the minister called, "now slide your right crutch out!"

Out came the other crutch.

"Now, Harry!" the minister called. "Say something so everyone can hear!"

The crowd was so quiet you could have heard the proverbial pin drop.

No answer.

"Harry," the minister called again, "don't be afraid! Speak up, man! Loud and clear!"

To which, Harry's tiny voice from behind the curtain said, "Fwed fell down."

★ ★ ★

"My Quaker neighbor finally got his lazy mule to pull the plow."

"I thought Quakers didn't believe in beating animals."

"He didn't. He threatened to trade it to a Southern Baptist."

★ ★ ★

First Young Man: What was that man asking you about?

Second Young Man: He wanted directions to the post office.

First Young Man: Don't you know who that was? That was the famous TV preacher, Bobby Johnson! He can show you the way to heaven!

Second Young Man: How can he do that if he doesn't even know the way to the post office?

★ ★ ★

The preacher had just admonished a regular churchgoer for not contributing enough money to the church.

"I'm sorry," the man answered, "but times are tough, and I have more debts than I can pay."

"But don't forget, you also have a debt to God," the preacher said.

"I know that," the man answered, "but He ain't pushing me like those other guys."

★ ★ ★

The wealthy elderly lady asked her minister if her recently deceased beloved pet dog could be buried in the church's cemetery with a religious service.

"I'm sorry," the minister answered, "but we Baptists don't perform religious burial services for dogs."

"That's too bad," the lady said. "I was prepared to donate ten thousand dollars for such a ceremony in the dog's name."

"Wait a minute," the minister answered. "You didn't tell me the dog was a Baptist."

Restaurants

Sign in restaurant window:

Good Food, Every Day But Sunday

★ ★ ★

"Hey, waitress, this chicken's got a wing missing."

"I know that. It was in a fight with another chicken last night."

"Well, take this one back and bring me the winner."

★ ★ ★

"Waiter, your sign says, 'Breakfast Anytime'. Is that right?"

"Yep. That's right."

"Good. I'll have waffles and bacon during the Civil War period."

★ ★ ★

"Waitress, this egg doesn't look fresh."

"Listen, mister, that egg is so fresh, the hen ain't even missed it yet."

★ ★ ★

"You've seen restaurants with a strolling violinist? That's the first one with a strolling rap singer."

★ ★ ★

"Waiter, is your chicken smothered in gravy?"

"I don't know. It's already dead when we get it."

★ ★ ★

"Waitress, what's all this stuff in the bottom of my cup?"
"How should I know? Do I look like a fortune teller?"

★ ★ ★

"Waiter, I can't eat this garbage. Send the cook out here."
"That won't help. He can't eat it, either."

★ ★ ★

"Waitress, gimme a hamburger and fries."
"Y' want it for here, or to go?"
"I'm hoping for both."

★ ★ ★

"How'd you like that new restaurant you went to last night?"
"Terrible. They got a sign that says, 'Please Wait for Hostess to Be Seated.'"
"So what?"
"So that hostess never did sit down."

★ ★ ★

"Waitress, what's this foreign object in my soup?"
"That's not foreign. Those things live around here."

★ ★ ★

"Waiter, I'm so hungry I could eat a horse."
"Well, you're in the right place."

★ ★ ★

"Hey, waitress, these grits are too runny."
"Those are your mashed potatoes."

★ ★ ★

The service in this restaurant is the worst I've ever seen, but I don't mind it because the food is so bad.

★ ★ ★

"Waitress, this doesn't look like chicken."

"It's chicken, all right. We lost the hatchet and had to stomp it to death."

★ ★ ★

"Don't tell my doctor I ordered this steak with all the trimmings."

"Does he have you on a special diet?"

"No, I owe him thirty-five dollars."

★ ★ ★

"Waiter, I can't tell whether this is apple pie or peach cobbler."

"Doesn't matter. They're both a dollar fifty."

★ ★ ★

"Waitress, I don't like the looks of this catfish."

"If it's looks you wanted, you shouldn't have ordered catfish."

★ ★ ★

"Waiter, bring me some more chicken."

"That'll cost you another four-ninety-five."

"But your sign says, 'All the Chicken You Can Eat, Four-Ninety-Five.'"

"See those chicken bones on your plate?"

"Yeah?"

"That is all you can eat for four-ninety-five."

★ ★ ★

"Waitress, does your cook have turkey breasts?"

"Yeah, but so what? He's wearing a T-shirt."

★ ★ ★

"I see your restaurant has sold twenty-five thousand hamburgers."

"Yeah, if it keeps up, we're gonna have to kill another cow."

★ ★ ★

"Hey, waitress, this dish is wet."
"That's your soup."

★ ★ ★

Last week I ordered something called "sushi." I swear, it tasted just like raw fish.

★ ★ ★

"Waiter, this tea is too weak."
"That's not tea, that's your water."
"In that case, it's too strong."

★ ★ ★

The last restaurant I was in was a terrible place. The eggs were old, the bread was stale, the meat was spoiled, and even the coat I walked out with was out of style.

★ ★ ★

The young fellow was applying for a job at the fast-food restaurant and the manager asked if he had any experience with fast food.
"Oh, sure," the young man answered. "I've eaten hundreds of Big Macs."

Rewards

"Is it true that you're offering a two-hundred-dollar reward for the safe return of your mother-in-law's trumpet?"
"Yes, and she thinks it's a wonderful gesture on my part."
"But isn't that an awfully big reward for returning a stolen trumpet?"
"Oh, not when it's at the bottom of Jones Lake tied to a concrete block with nylon rope."

Running

The bartender couldn't help noticing the stranger in the jogging outfit at the bar.

"Are you a jogger?" he asked.

"Not really," the man answered. "A week ago, my doctor told me to start running ten miles a day, so I have been."

"Do you feel any better?"

"Oh, I feel great," the man said. "Trouble is, I'm seventy miles from home."

Sales/Salespeople

"I see you've lost weight since you started your new job. Did your boss put you on a diet?"

"No, he put me on commission."

★ ★ ★

"Well, how did your first day as a salesman turn out?"

"Lousy. I only got two orders."

"That doesn't sound so bad, considering it was your very first day."

"Oh, no? The first order was to get out, and the second was to stay out."

Scams/Swindles

"This wristwatch you sold me doesn't work."

"Of course not. That's why I sold it so cheap. I didn't say it worked!"

"But how do you expect me to know what time it is?"

"Oh, for Pete's sake! Just ask somebody!"

★ ★ ★

"Where's your new wristwatch?"

"I had to throw it away."

"What? You said that watch was guaranteed to be shock-resistant, waterproof, anti-magnetic, dust-proof, rust-proof, crush-proof, shatter-resistant, and absolutely accurate to a minute per year!"

"Yeah, it was all that."

"Well, what on earth happened to it?"

"It caught fire."

★ ★ ★

"That bottle of magic potion you sold me was supposed to make me smarter . . . I'm beginning to think I was swindled."

"See there?! You're smarter already!"

School

Young Boy to Teacher: Listen, Miss Gray, I don't wanna scare you, but my dad said if I don't get better grades on my next report card, somebody's gonna be in very big trouble.

★ ★ ★

"He used to take his dog to school every day, but he finally had to stop."

"How come?"

"The dog graduated."

★ ★ ★

"I understand he was quite a cut-up back in grade school."

"I'll say! His third grade teacher used to charge a three-dollar cover and a two-drink minimum."

★ ★ ★

Teacher: Spell "cat."

Student: House cat or pole cat?

Teacher: What's the difference?

Student: If you don't know the difference between a house cat and a pole cat, you've got no business teaching.

★ ★ ★

"When you were a boy, did you miss school a lot?"
"Not a bit."

★ ★ ★

"What's your brother going to be when he graduates from college?"
"Oh, I'd say about fifty."

Science

Science is advancing so fast, inventors aren't even bothering with building better mousetraps. They're building better mice.

Secrets

Women can keep a secret every bit as well as men. It just takes more of them to do it.

★ ★ ★

She can keep a secret just fine, but the people she tells it to can't.

Self-Made People

The trouble with being a self-made man is, you have to take the blame.

★ ★ ★

"Daddy, my new boyfriend says he's a self-made man."
"Well, at least he's willing to accept blame."

★ ★ ★

I'm a self-made man, but if I had it all to do over again, I'd call in outside help.

Shopping

Woman to Store Clerk: I want to buy a shotgun for my husband.
Clerk: Did he let you know what kind he likes?
Woman: No. He doesn't even know I'm gonna shoot him.

★ ★ ★

My uncle was hurt while he was shopping. The dumpster lid fell on him.

Show Business

"She's married to her acting career."
"In that case, she should sue for non-support."

Sincerity

She is definitely not a sincere person. She married John while she was engaged to Frank so she could have a place to meet Billy in order to make Tommy jealous in front of Harold.

Singing/Singers

"For a western singer, she has a very big repertoire."
"Yeah. Must be the sourdough bread."

★ ★ ★

"Can I borrow one of your microphone cords?"
"Sure. I've got a five-footer and a fifteen-footer. How long do you want it?"
"For a pretty good while. I'm going on the road."

★ ★ ★

"Why did you talk her into switching to playing the trumpet instead of playing the piano?"
"Because when she's playing the trumpet, she can't sing."

★ ★ ★

That girl even laughs out of key.

★ ★ ★

"Did you hear her sing that sad song?"
"Sad? The way she sings, it was pitiful."

★ ★ ★

"I understand she had her singing voice insured for fifty thousand dollars."
"What did she do with the money?"

★ ★ ★

"He sings to kill time."
"He's certainly using a lethal weapon."

★ ★ ★

"Did you hear about my latest album?"
"Yes, I did. What's your side of the story?"

★ ★ ★

He sang two songs last night: the first because someone asked him to, and the second to prove he wasn't afraid of them.

★ ★ ★

"Can you sing *a cappella*?"
"Maybe. Hum a few bars."

★ ★ ★

"Grady Renfro sold his guitar, quit his band, and got a job at the furniture factory."
"But I thought Grady was a singer?"
"That's exactly the same mistake he made."

Sleep/Sleeping

"Did you sleep well?"
"No, I made several mistakes."

Smoking

"He's a tobacco farmer."
"Does he grow cigars or cigarettes?"

★ ★ ★

"I hear your brother's trying to quit smoking."
"Yeah, he got some of those plastic filters that fit on the end of your cigarettes. They're supposed to help you taper off."
"How's he doing?"
"Well, he still smokes, but now he can suck-start the lawn mower."

★ ★ ★

"I see you've started rolling your own cigarettes."
"Yeah, my doctor said I should get more exercise."

Society

"She thinks she's the cream of society."
"Somebody should tell her she's starting to curdle."

Songs

"Y'know, I've always wanted to get to know Amazing Grace a lot better."
"It's a beautiful song, all right."
"Not the song. I'm talking about Grace Grabowski."

★ ★ ★

In Nashville, when we got the news about war in the Middle East, we all gathered to protect the Grand Ole Opry from terrorists—so they couldn't cut off our nasal twangs.

★ ★ ★

"Did you hear the song I wrote because my sweetheart ran off?"
"Yes, I did."
"What do you think?"
"Next time let your sweetheart write the songs and you run off."

★ ★ ★

"I just wrote a song about an Indian that's a sure-fire country music hit."
"An Indian? What's the name of it?"
"A Sioux Named Boy."

★ ★ ★

"... Then in 1427, I wrote ..."

"I've written songs for Waylon Jennings, Tina Turner, Frank Sinatra, Prince, and Madonna."

"My goodness! Have all those stars sung your songs?"

"I didn't say they sang them. I said I wrote them."

★ ★ ★

"How many country music songwriters does it take to change a lightbulb?"

"Six. One to put in the new bulb, and five to write about how much they miss the old one."

Spot Remover

"Yesterday, I spilled a bottle of spot remover on my best huntin' dog."

"Is he all right?"

"I don't know. I can't find 'im. I can hear 'im, but I can't find 'im."

★ ★ ★

"I bought a bottle of spot remover, and my husband thought it was liquor."

"What happened?"

"He drank it, and dropped out of sight."

Stage Fright

"Do you ever get stage fright?"

"No, I'm not afraid of the stage. It's the audience that scares me."

States

"How was your trip to New Jersey?"

"Well, a mugger stopped me and said, 'Gimme your money, or I'll blow your brains out.'"

"What did you do?"

"I told him to go ahead and shoot. He was so shocked, he ran away."

"Wow! He told you to give him your money or he'd blow your brains out, and you told him to go ahead and shoot?"

"Yeah. You don't need brains to live in New Jersey, but you can't get along without money."

★ ★ ★

"Why is New Jersey called 'The Garden State'?"

"Because everybody's guardin' their house, guardin' their car, guardin' their kids . . ."

Rejected State Mottos

Mottos you're not likely to see on certain license plates

Alabama: Literasy Ain't Everything
Arkansas: At Least We're Not Oklahoma
Georgia: Freedom Schmeedom
Illinois: Gateway To Iowa
Kansas: Orville Redenbacher for President
Kentucky: Tobacco Is a Vegetable
Maryland: Birthplace of the Indianapolis Colts
Minnesota: For Sale
Montana: Land of the Big Sky, and Very Little Else
New Jersey: You Have the Right to Remain Silent, You Have the Right to an Attorney
New Mexico: Lizards Make Excellent Pets
North Carolina: Five Million People, Fifteen Last Names
Ohio: Don't Judge Us by Cleveland

Pennsylvania: Cook With Coal
South Dakota: Closer Than North Dakota
Tennessee: The Educashun State
Texas: ¡Sí! ¡Hablo Inglés!
Utah: Our Jesus Is Better Than Your Jesus
West Virginia: Marijuana: Cholesterol Free

Statistics

Statistics show that the average person believes he is above average, but he's not.

★ ★ ★

Statistics have proven beyond a doubt that statistics are wrong about half the time.

★ ★ ★

I don't believe in statistics. Last winter, I camped out and built a fire and fell asleep next to it. When I woke up, my frontside was burning up hot and sweaty, but my backside was freezing cold. But according to statistics, on the whole, I felt just right.

Stock Brokers

"I used to be a broker."
"Isn't that something to do with the stock market?"
"Yeah. It's what you get if you mess with it."

★ ★ ★

"To get rich in the stock market, buy stock, and when it goes up, sell it."
"But what if it doesn't go up?"
"Don't buy it."

Striptease Dancing/Strippers

"His uncle told him to never go to a strip show because he might see something he shouldn't but he went anyway."
"And did he see something he shouldn't?"
"Yep. He saw his uncle."

★ ★ ★

"Preacher Jones seems very upset lately."
"That's because he's got mixed emotions."
"Why does he have mixed emotions?"
"His daughter got very rich and very famous as a stripper. Now he can't decide if he's proud of her or ashamed of her."

Stupidity

"You know, nowadays, a man can get rich and famous without having a brain in his head."
"*You* didn't."

★ ★ ★

She is sooo dumb . . .

. . . she thinks "guerrilla warfare" is a food fight at a zoo.

. . . she thinks *Roe v. Wade* are two different ways to cross a river.

. . . the last time I saw her, I said "hello" and she was stuck for an answer.

. . . she doesn't know the difference between a political party and a stag party.

. . . she thinks Plato is a distant planet.

. . . if she were a lighthouse, she'd have a fifteen-watt beacon.

Success/Successful People

The more successful you become, the less you get called "Hey, you!"

★ ★ ★

Of course, you never know what you *can't* do until you try, either.

Superstition

Always remember: It's bad luck to be superstitious.

★ ★ ★

"My fortune teller told me to beware of being swindled."
"Don't you know better than to believe anything a fortune teller says?"
"But it came true."
"It did?"
"Yeah . . . she charged me eighty-five dollars."

★ ★ ★

"A couple of years ago, my fortune teller told me I had a big, expensive automobile in my future."
"Was it true?"
"Yep. Next day, I got hit by a Lincoln."

★ ★ ★

Wife to Husband: You're lucky to have a wife like me.
Husband: What makes you say that?
Wife: When you lost all your money in that car wash business, I stuck by you; when you went broke in that moonshine business, I stuck by you; and when you lost everything in that pyramid scheme, I was right there beside you. All that ought to tell you something!
Husband: Yeah. It tells me you're a jinx.

★ ★ ★

"Is it true that you're a professional palm reader and fortune teller?"

"Yes."

"How's business?"

"Oh. . . . Medium."

★ ★ ★

"I had a fortune teller read my palm and check my lifeline."

"What'd she have to say?"

"She said I should try to live a cleaner life."

Swimming/Swimsuits

Police Chief to Patrolman: Let me get this straight. You say you saw three beautiful young girls undressing out by the creek?

Patrolman: That's right, chief.

Chief: And after they undressed, they waded into the creek to go swimming?

Patrolman: Yep, and that's when I arrested them for swimming in an unauthorized area.

Chief: But why didn't you arrest them before they took off all their clothes?

Patrolman: Well, I wasn't sure there was such a thing as *attempted* swimming in an unauthorized area.

★ ★ ★

"Sally Renfro was downtown in her string bikini."

"Wow! She's lucky she wasn't arrested for indecent exposure."

"No chance of that. She looked plenty decent!"

★ ★ ★

A young boy was skinny dipping in his favorite swimming hole when a troop of Girl Scouts happened along and spotted him.

Laughing playfully, they decided to sit down next to the boy's clothes and have a leisurely lunch, trapping him in the water.

But the boy was familiar with the creek, and he knew where there was an old washtub someone had discarded on the bottom. He found the tub, used it to hide himself, and marched up the bank to fetch his clothes.

The Girl Scouts laughed even harder as he approached, and he decided to give them a piece of his mind. He asked angrily, "Do you girls know what I think?"

"Yes, we do," answered one of the girls who could stop laughing long enough to speak. "You think there's a bottom in that rusty old washtub!"

★ ★ ★

"Say, I saw your wife at the beach in her new bathing suit."
"What color was it?"
"I don't know. She was facing the other way."

★ ★ ★

Her new bikini reminds me of that old saying: A place for everything, and everything in its place.

★ ★ ★

"That's some sexy new bikini she's wearing!"
"Yeah, it's keeping everybody warm but her."

Taxis

"Driver, can't you go any faster?"
"Sure, but the boss says I have to stay with the cab."

★ ★ ★

"The last time I was in a taxi, we were going down a long hill and the driver suddenly yelled, 'The brakes are gone! I can't stop!'"

"What did you do?"

"What else? I told him to turn off the meter."

Telephones

"Operator, I want to report an accident! A truck loaded with dynamite just crashed into a truck loaded with fireworks!"

"Good heavens! Where's the accident?"

"On Jefferson Boulevard, Main Street, Clinton Avenue, the Johnson Freeway, Walnut Street, and Circle Drive."

★ ★ ★

First Young Woman: I'm getting fed up with obscene telephone calls!

Second Young Woman: I didn't know you were getting obscene telephone calls.

First Young Woman: I'm not getting them—I'm making them.

★ ★ ★

"Operator, how much does it cost to call long distance?"

"That depends on where you're calling."

"I'm callin' my Uncle Ralph."

"Well, where does your Uncle Ralph live?"

"Oh, 'bout half a mile from my house."

"From your house? Sir, if you're calling only a half-mile from your house, that's not a long distance call."

"Wow! That's good news! In that case, I'll call my cousin, too!"

"Where is your cousin?"

"He's living at my house."

"At your house?"

"Yeah, he's taking care of things while I'm here in Europe."

★ ★ ★

"Operator, I want to call my cousin, Helen, in Churubusco, Indiana."

"How do you spell that?"

"H-e-l-e-n."

"Not 'Helen.' How do you spell 'Churubusco'?"

"Operator, if I knew how to spell that, I'd write her a letter."

★ ★ ★

"Say, little cutie, what's your telephone number?"

"Oh, it's in the book."

"Great! What's your name?"

"That's in the book, too."

Tennis

Remember, you can't play tennis without raising a racket.

Thirst

I am so thirsty, I'd have to staple on a postage stamp.

Traffic

"I've never seen Grandpa so mad. The state's decided to put a four-lane highway right through the middle of his pasture."

"Why is he so mad about that?"

"He thinks he'll have to run down and open the gate every time a car comes along."

★ ★ ★

"In New York City, a man gets hit with a car every forty-eight minutes."

"Wow! If I was him, I'd get off the street!"

★ ★ ★

"My cousin in New York City finally stopped complaining about finding a parking place."

"What happened?"

"He bought a parked car."

Travel

Man to Ticket Agent: I want to buy a bus ticket for Norwald.
Ticket Agent, Searching Book: Norwald? Let me find that. Hmm . . . never heard of it. Let me see . . . Norwald. I don't see Norwald listed, and I can't find it on the map. Just where is Norwald, anyway?
Man: Over there. He's my brother-in-law.

★ ★ ★

"If I could afford it, I'd like to travel."
"Don't worry. I'm sure the neighbors will chip in."

Travel Tips

Helpful Hints for the inexperienced traveler:

- Be very suspicious if the advertised price of a Caribbean cruise includes the phrase "Free Ammo."

- Consider carefully before visiting a country where the license plate motto is *Die American Pig*.

- Keep in mind that, in the Middle East, the phrase "half off" on a hotel room has nothing to do with price.

- There is no legitimate reason for a travel agent to need to know if you have experience in jungle warfare.

- If you find yourself in Iran, do not use the word *blankethead*.

- On a trip to Canada, your travel agent should not charge you for an interpreter.

- In Denmark, those mannequins in storefront windows are not mannequins.

- While in the Vatican, do not refer to St. Peter as "Petey-Boy."
- Do not board a cruise ship if passengers are being issued oars.
- Avoid any Latin American Tour named *Bay of Pigs, Two.*
- In South America, say no to anyone wanting you to deliver a suitcase of powdered sugar to their grandmother in Miami.
- Legitimate travel agents do not dress in foreign military uniforms.
- If you find yourself in South Africa—and you're black—skip your usual late-night jog.

Trees

"My new boyfriend grows apples."
"Don't talk crazy. Trees grow apples."

Trucks

"What was Old Man Sweeney doing with those goats in the back of his pickup truck this morning?"
"Oh, I'd say about forty miles an hour."

Twins/Triplets

"I hear you had a date with the Thompson twins."
"I sure did."
"Did you have a good time?"
"Yes and no."

★ ★ ★

"I hear Mrs. Johnson had triplets. That only happens once every six-hundred-thousand times."
"Good heavens! When did she have time to do housework?"

★ ★ ★

Did you hear about the Siamese twins joined at the hip?
They had to commute to England so the other one could drive.

★ ★ ★

"My brother's finally divorcing those Siamese twins he married."
"How come?"
"On these cold winter nights, he can't stand all those cold feet on his back."

★ ★ ★

"I hear Susan is a twin."
"That's right."
"How do people know which is which?"
"Her brother has a mustache."

Ugliness

"My new girl's got everything a man could want."
"Yeah, including a nice beard."

★ ★ ★

First Man: What's your hurry?
Second Man: I'm lookin' for the doctor to help my wife. She looks terrible!
First Man: I'll help you find him—my wife's no beauty, either.

★ ★ ★

He's so ugly . . .

. . . he looks like he fell out of an Ugly Tree and hit every limb on the way down.

. . . dogs won't come to him in public.

. . . he looks like he drove down Ugly Highway and hit every chuckhole.

. . . dogs are afraid to bark at him.

. . . he has to sneak up on a glass to get a drink.

★ ★ ★

Ed: What's the difference between a dog and a fox?
Fred: Oh, about five stiff drinks.

★ ★ ★

His sister has so much body hair, her parents have to ground her during hunting season.

Weather

It was so cold today, I saw a lawyer with his hands in his own pockets.

Weight

"She claims she used to have an hourglass figure."
"Well, time marches on."

★ ★ ★

I don't want to say that man is fat, but he can take a shower without getting his feet wet.

★ ★ ★

"He claims his girlfriend just won a city-wide contest."
"No wonder. She's the widest girl in the city."

★ ★ ★

I guess you could say she's got an hourglass figure, but it's 'way past noon.

★ ★ ★

My mother-in-law went to that new department store. I
don't want to say she's too heavy, but she spent a good part of
the afternoon taking the escalator to the second floor.
'Course, she made up the time on her trip back.

★ ★ ★

I don't want to insinuate that she's too skinny, but she and I
were swimming the other day, and there must have been a
dozen places on her where I could hang my towel.

★ ★ ★

He's got Dixie Dunlap disease—his belly's done lapped over
his belt.

★ ★ ★

She claims she's not overweight at all—she's just two and a
half feet too short.

★ ★ ★

"Is it true that his new girlfriend is overweight?"
"Let's just say that, around her, a 'megabyte' has nothing to
do with a computer."

★ ★ ★

"She got that hat from over in London and that purse from
over in Paris and those shoes from over in Italy."
"Maybe. But she got that figure from over in the kitchen."

★ ★ ★

He's so thin, when he drinks tomato juice he looks like a
thermometer.

★ ★ ★

If it wasn't for her kneecaps and Adam's apple, she
wouldn't have any shape at all.

★ ★ ★

Wife to Husband: You used to say I had a million-dollar figure.
Husband: That was before you made all those bad invest-
ments.

★ ★ ★

That man is so skinny you can count how many olives he's
eaten.

★ ★ ★

"I weighed myself on one of those scales that tells your fortune, and it said, 'You are good-looking, intelligent, and well-
liked by everyone you meet.'"
"I'll bet it got your weight wrong, too."

★ ★ ★

He was so fat, when he got his shoes shined, he had to take
the man's word for it.

Welfare

"Not having a job, and living off welfare like you do, do you
ever have any trouble getting the basic necessities of life?"
"I sure do. And half the time, when I do get it, it ain't fit to
drink."

Widows/Widowers

"George has his eye on the Widow Martin."
"He does?"
"Yeah, he asked her if he could take her husband's place."
"What'd she say?"
"She said it was fine with her, if he could arrange it with the
undertaker."

Wishes/Wishing

"The trouble with you is, you're always wishing for something you don't have."
"What else is there to wish for?"

★ ★ ★

"If you had only one wish, what would it be?"
"I'd wish all my wishes would come true."

Women's Liberation

"Grandma, when you and Grandpa had your first baby, did Grandpa ever handle the middle-of-the-night feeding?"
"No. I always did that."
"That must have been before you had women's liberation."
"No, it was before we had baby bottles."

★ ★ ★

"Nowadays, a woman can be anything she wants."
"I guess none of 'em want to be an uncle."

★ ★ ★

"I hear your aunt had eleven children."
"She sure did."
"Why didn't she go ahead and have an even dozen?"
"She figured it might interfere with her career."

Writers

"I heard she made a fortune from a story she made up."
"Who'd she sell it to?"
"A jury."

★ ★ ★

"If Shakespeare were alive today, he would still be regarded as a remarkable man."

"I'll say! He'd be over three hundred years old!"

★ ★ ★

"Didn't you say your son was a professional author?"

"No, not quite. I said, every time he writes a letter, it's for money."